6-5-75

THE POETRY OF ROBERT LOWELL

SYDNEY STUDIES IN LITERATURE

JAMES JOYCE'S *ULYSSES*
by Clive Hart

JANE AUSTEN'S *EMMA*
by J. F. Burrows

THE MAJOR POEMS OF JOHN KEATS
by Norman Talbot

MILTON'S *PARADISE LOST*
by Michael Wilding

THE POETRY OF ROBERT LOWELL
by Vivian Smith

A READING OF SHAKESPEARE'S *ANTONY AND CLEOPATRA*
by A. P. Riemer

SHAKESPEARE'S *HAMLET*
by Derick R. Marsh

THE POETRY OF
ROBERT LOWELL

VIVIAN SMITH

Lecturer in English
University of Sydney

SYDNEY UNIVERSITY PRESS

SYDNEY UNIVERSITY PRESS

Press Building, University of Sydney

UNITED KINGDOM, EUROPE, MIDDLE EAST, AFRICA, CARIBBEAN
Prentice/Hall International, International Book Distributors Ltd,
Hemel Hempstead, England

NORTH AND SOUTH AMERICA
International Scholarly Book Services, Inc., Portland, Oregon

To Sybille

First published 1974

© Vivian Smith 1974

Library of Congress Catalog Card Number 73-88749

National Library of Australia registry card number and
ISBN 0 424 06510 X

This book is supported by money from
THE ELEANOR SOPHIA WOOD BEQUEST

Printed in Australia at The Griffin Press, Adelaide

CONTENTS

PREFACE

This study is designed to introduce the poetry of Robert Lowell to new readers. Teaching the poetry of Robert Lowell over the last few years, I have found that he is a poet who appeals greatly to students, but one who needs much interpretation before he can be properly understood and evaluated. I have also found that there is nothing that frustrates and irritates readers and students so much as being given evaluations of poems which they have not yet fully understood. They want to earn and acquire their judgement through personal understanding. The basic Lowell problem for the beginner is the simple one of comprehension. This is then very much a groundwork book—a reader's guide—containing a large amount of information, interpretation and explication, and I hope stimulus and suggestion for further thought and reading. It is basically a commentary on particular poems, offering a number of interpretations and readings of poems that have not been commented on before, though of course covering the essentials and commenting on poems that have already received much attention. Given the state of Lowell studies and the fact that Lowell is still in mid-career, this seems to me the best service that one can offer at present. The aesthetic pleasure to be derived from Lowell's work is not often stressed, but it has been my main concern in the following critical appreciations.

There is a particular tendency in writing on Lowell—much of whose work is autobiographical—for the interest to shift from the work of art to the man. Lowell himself is such an interesting figure that there is always a temptation to get caught up in the larger cultural issues he represents. I have particularly tried to avoid that temptation in the following pages, and I have tried to look at the poems as works of art which have an existence independent of the author's life or of any thesis that they might be used to support.

There are particular problems to be faced in discussing the work of a living writer, though these can be exaggerated. The main one, in my view, is that the body of work is not yet finished and relationships that may appear in the total *oeuvre* are not yet clear.

7

Any statements made about the work as a whole can only apply to the stage it was at when the statement was made. There are other problems associated with the texts themselves. Lowell is a writer who has published several different versions of the one poem, and poems are constantly being revised from one edition to another.

If there are difficulties and drawbacks in writing about a living writer, there are also compensations. Contemporaneity can be a mixed blessing, but there is something exciting about reading the work of a major living author written in and out of the circumstances of the world we live in; an author who is responding to the past and the present at the same time as ourselves and writing about the problems and issues that immediately concern us.

At the time of writing this I note that Lowell's reputation seems to be undergoing some depressions and fluctuations. There is a sense of reassessment in the air. The early work is no longer considered as highly as it once was; misgivings are being expressed about the more recent poems; there is a feeling that Lowell has been overvalued. Such fluctuations of opinion are inevitable. I had better say at once that I consider Lowell a major poet. I do not of course mean—as the following pages show—that he is beyond criticism. Much of his work seems to me flawed and incomplete, but he has a scope, a range, a control and an ambition that are those of a major poet. His work at its best gives us that sense of truth of human experience and authentic wholeness that is a mark of great poetry.

The amount of critical attention that Lowell has received bears testimony to the fact that he is a poet whose work calls for constant reassessment and evaluation. His abundant productivity, his capacity for constant renewal and yet the consistency of his central preoccupations point to the creation of a major poet. Edmund Wilson remarked some time ago that Lowell, like Auden, is one of the few modern poets who have been able to sustain a body of work, a poetic career, on the scale of the major poetic talents of the nineteenth century. His output, apart from the ten volumes of poetry, includes his verse translation of Racine's *Phèdre* (1961) and his *Prometheus Bound* (1969), derived from Aeschylus. His first dramatic work *The Old Glory* (1966) consisted of three plays 'Benito Cereno', 'My Kinsman, Major Molineux', and 'Endecott and the Red Cross', based on stories by Hawthorne and a novella by Melville. It is interesting to note that Lowell has consciously and consistently eschewed the writing of criticism on any scale, and in this he differs from contemporaries like W. H. Auden and Randall Jarrell. His critical pieces, like those of Hopkins, Williams and Jarrell, are tributes from one artist to another, often consciously

8

revealing much of Lowell's sense of indebtedness to the poets he writes of. His criticism has none of the detachment of the academic writer. His poetic career has been a vigorous and dedicated one, and like the career of Yeats and Auden, for instance, it has had constant public significance on the level of politics and art. There is already a welter of opinion about Lowell, many suggestive comments and aperçus and some very learned studies and articles. Nevertheless there does not exist an adequate basis of sustained reading and interpretation of individual poems and I hope the following pages will help to fill this gap.

Anybody writing of Robert Lowell and his work must be conscious of a deep debt to the pioneer studies of Hugh B. Staples, *Robert Lowell; The First Twenty Years* (1962) and Jerome Mazzaro, *The Poetic Themes of Robert Lowell* (1965). Since the appearance of these first book-length studies other volumes have appeared, most notably the chapter devoted to Lowell in M. L. Rosenthal, *The New Poets: American and British Poetry since World War II* (1967), Patrick Cosgrave, *The Public Poetry of Robert Lowell* (1970), Philip Cooper, *The Autobiographical Myth of Robert Lowell* (1970) and Richard Fein's *Robert Lowell* (1971). My debts to these different books, including the stimulus of disagreement, will be apparent in the following pages. As well, there are many articles and chapters of varying length in the various volumes and symposia devoted to American poetry which deal with aspects of Lowell's work, his themes and preoccupations. The most important are listed in the Select Bibliography.

University of Sydney   *Vivian Smith*
May, 1973

This study was prepared for the press before the appearance of *The Dolphin, For Lizzie and Harriet* and *History*, the new volumes which revise, recast and add to the poems already published in *Notebook*. I have thus not been able to take the revisions into account or to refer to the new biographical information that they contain.

December, 1973   *V.S.*

ACKNOWLEDGEMENTS

The following presses kindly granted copyright permissions: Harcourt Brace Jovanovich, Inc., New York and George Allen & Unwin Ltd, London for quotations from R. P. Blackmur, *Language as Gesture*; Harcourt Brace Jovanovich, Inc. and Faber and Faber Ltd, London for extracts from Robert Lowell, *Poems 1938-1949*; Farrar, Straus & Giroux, Inc., New York and Faber and Faber Ltd for extracts from Robert Lowell, *Life Studies* (copyright © 1956, 1959 by Robert Lowell), *For the Union Dead* (copyright © 1956, 1960, 1961, 1962, 1963, 1964 by Robert Lowell), *Phaedra* (copyright © 1960, 1961 by Robert Lowell), *Near the Ocean* (copyright © 1963, 1965, 1966, 1967 by Robert Lowell), and *Notebook* (copyright © 1967, 1968, 1969, 1970 by Robert Lowell); and *The Nation*, New York for an extract from a review by Robert Lowell of William Carlos Williams, *Paterson*.

INTRODUCTION

Robert Trail Spence Lowell was born in Boston on 1 March 1917, and the first significant fact about his life is that he comes from one of the important American dynastic families. The history of his family covers that of his whole country. His mother, Charlotte Winslow, was descended from Edward Winslow, one of the Pilgrim Fathers, and General John Stark. His father, Commander R. T. S. Lowell, USN, trained as a naval officer and belonged to a well-known family of intellectuals and writers, his father having been an Episcopal minister and Headmaster of St Mark's School. James Russell Lowell (1819-91) was his great great uncle; Amy Lowell, one of the leading American poets just before World War I, was a distant cousin. Lowell's childhood, which he has described in his autobiographical prose work '91 Revere Street', was spent on Beacon Hill and at St Mark's School. Richard Eberhardt, the poet, taught there. In 1935 Lowell went as a student to Harvard, but after the first year there left to study with John Crowe Ransom at Kenyon College in Gambier, Ohio. He majored in classics, graduating *summa cum laude*. These were important years in Lowell's life. In 1937 he spent three months at the home of Allen Tate at Monteagle, Tennessee and Tate was to prove an influential guide and stimulus in his life. Tate was a highly learned poet; he consistently asserted that a poem was a technological object that stood independently of the poet's life or feelings; that poetry was a craft that could be learned and mastered. Tate's emphasis on form ' . . . to write in meters, but to make the meters look hard and make them hard to write'[1] was a decisive influence on Lowell's early work as it was on the development of formalism generally in the 'forties.

In 1940 Lowell entered the Roman Catholic Church and married the novelist Jean Stafford. For a while he taught English literature at Kenyon College and then from 1941-2 worked as an editorial assistant for the Catholic publishing firm Sheed and Ward in New York City. At the beginning of America's entry into the second world war Lowell had attempted to enlist but had been rejected

1 See Jay Martin, *Robert Lowell*, Minneapolis 1970, p. 9.

because of ill health. In 1943, however, he was indicted for failure to obey the Selective Service Act. At his trial he explained that he objected to the Allied bombing of civilians in Europe. He was sentenced to serve a year and a day in a Federal prison but was released after about six months.

Lowell's first book of poems, *Land of Unlikeness*, appeared in 1944; *Lord Weary's Castle* appeared in 1946 and was awarded the Pulitzer Prize for poetry and the American Academy of Arts and Letters Prize. This recognition resulted in his appointment as consultant in Poetry at the Library of Congress from 1947-8. Divorced from Jean Stafford in June 1948, Lowell married the writer and critic Elizabeth Hardwick in July 1949. In 1950 Faber and Faber published his *Poems 1938-1949*; his father died in the same year. Lowell spent three years in Europe from 1950-3—mostly in Salzburg and Rome. In 1951 he published *The Mills of the Kavanaughs* which may be said to bring to an end the first phase of his career. His mother died in 1954 and for a while during this period Lowell suffered a number of nervous breakdowns which seriously threatened his sanity. Then in 1959 appeared *Life Studies: New Poems and an Autobiographical Fragment*, the work which marked Lowell's breakthrough into a new world of style and experience. This work received the National Book Award and inaugurates a new phase in Lowell's writing.

Lowell's work, like that of any major figure, falls naturally into its own broad chronological phases, with overlappings, continuities and transitions. It has its own inner coherence and imaginative logic and inevitability. While his most recent poetry is his most acclaimed, especially for its diffidence and modesty of tone, his earlier formalistic verse should not be underestimated in comparison with the later work. The hard-won freedom and seemingly effortless flexibility of his most recent poetry would be inconceivable without the years of involved formalism that preceded it. His work in fact plots a graph from the formalism of the 'forties to the open form poetry of the 'fifties and 'sixties.

Poems 1938-49

The first general impression conveyed by Lowell's earlier poems is one of unrelieved violence and fury, a rage of energy which is concentrated and highlighted by the formalism of the poems as a whole. Lowell's first mature poems started to appear during the formalist 1940s under the influence of poets like Allen Tate and John Crowe Ransom, and he has recorded how deliberately he set out to write poems which were as technically intricate and formalized as possible:

> [Tate and I] both liked rather formal, difficult poems, and we were reading particularly the Sixteenth and Seventeenth centuries. In the evening we'd read aloud, and we started a card catalogue of what we'd make for the anthology. And then we started writing. It seems to me we took old models like Drayton's Ode—Tate wrote a poem called 'The Young Proconsuls of the Air' in that stanza. I think there's a trick to formal poetry. Most poetry is very formal, but when a modern poet is formal he gets more attention for it than old poets did. Somehow we've tried to make it look difficult. For example, Shelley can just rattle off terza rima by the page, and it's very smooth, doesn't seem an obstruction to him—you sometimes wish it were more difficult. Well, someone does that today and in modern style it looks as though he's wrestling with every line and may be pushed into confusion, as though he's having a real struggle with form and content. Marks of that are in the finished poem. And I think both Tate and I felt that we wanted our formal patterns to seem a hardship and something that we couldn't rattle off easily.[1]

The other general impression the poems convey is through their basic imagery which tends to be abrasive, elemental—images of winter, the sea, iron and stone, destroyed or decaying trees, suffering animals, and destruction and waste seem to predominate in a first reading. Closer acquaintance shows how these are sometimes tempered and reinforced by other images evoking gentleness and vulnerability, frailty and delicately persisting endurance. But the

[1] Robert Lowell, as interviewed by Frederick Seidel, reprinted in T. Parkinson (ed.), *Robert Lowell, A Collection of Critical Essays*, Englewood Cliffs 1968, p. 17.

first impression is a lasting and revealing one, and not to be dissolved by later qualifications.

Thematically the poems in *Poems 1938-1949* fall into three broad groups: poems on the family, poems on history, and poems specifically about the war in Europe 1939-45. This is just a rough and ready grouping, of course, because many of these themes come together in the one poem; most of the poems use religious, usually apocalyptic imagery, and a variety of classical allusions. In some of these poems Lowell tries to merge the two strands of western culture rather in the manner of a Renaissance poet—a Ronsard or a D'Aubigné—rifling poetic sources and resources at need. Formally, the poems also fall into well defined genres and modes: elegies predominate ('The Quaker Graveyard in Nantucket', 'In Memory of Arthur Winslow', 'Winter in Dunbarton' and 'Mary Winslow' are the outstanding examples); and Lowell displays his technical skill in sonnets, adapted translations (which he always refers to— borrowing the term from Dryden—as imitations), narratives and monologues which adopt the open couplets of Browning, applying them to contemporary or historical situations. In the early work there is a strong sense of an ambitious and strenuous poet trying out his paces and determined to master as many recalcitrant forms as possible.

Lowell's range of reference is uncommonly wide, moving from the ancient world through various aspects of American and European history to semi-private references to the members of his own family, his own experiences and friendships.

The first poem 'The Exile's Return' is a dramatic atmospheric piece which takes the traditional wanderer's return theme and uses it as an image for the state of every man and the state of the world after World War II. The situation imagined is that which will face a Displaced Person when he returns to his homeland (the Rhineland) after its occupation by the liberating army (American). The opening images are those of winter and war with the victorious army winning back the lost war-torn city. The wanderer is reminded that he will not see any aspects of the remembered or expected past ('the strutting children' or 'the peg-leg chancellor') when he returns; but after the violence of war and the bleakness of winter there are already signs of hope and spring:

> . . . already lily-stands
> Burgeon the risen Rhineland, and a rough
> Cathedral lifts its eye. Pleasant enough,
> *Voi ch'entrate*, and your life is in your hands.

The ending is ambiguous, affirmative but highly tempered; the images of Christian hope are controlled by the reference to Dante and the words written over the gate to Hell. The return is pleasant enough, but it is a return to Hell, to a war-ravaged place, and what will happen depends on the self and its resources.

The title of 'The Holy Innocents' refers to the Feast of the Holy Innocents, 28 December, which commemorates the children of Bethlehem who were killed by Herod in an attempt to destroy the infant Jesus.[2] Patrick Cosgrave, in his acute and very full commentary on this poem,[3] claims that there are two lines of analogy moving through the poem: the outer analogy between the team of oxen struggling up the hill and the year 1945 struggling up the hill of history; and the analogy between the oxen— simple beasts of burden—and the simple followers of Christ. The oxen

> . . . are the undefiled by woman—their
> Sorrow is not the sorrow of this world:
> King Herod shrieking vengeance at the curled
> Up knees of Jesus choking in the air.

They represent the followers of Christ who are alienated from the world of man and, in a special way, from the world of twentieth-century man. 'The world is the burden the followers of Christ bear, as the oxen pull the cart' as Cosgrave puts it.[4]

But it is very difficult for the reader to accept this account without question. There does not seem to be any double focus of the central analogy but rather the total poetic attention is on the phenomenon of the oxen and the articulation of responses they arouse in an awareness tuned to the twentieth century. It is part of the poem's ambience that one senses a reflection of the human condition in the oxen, but it is hard to feel that there is a real justification for positing a central analogy. The poem draws its basic imagery from traditional Biblical associations and Christian iconography where the ox is associated with Christian submissiveness and the spirit of self-sacrifice. The last three lines, while they pick up the usual Christian suggestions of the silence and omnipotence of God, are also, like the last line of 'The Quaker Graveyard in Nantucket', ambiguous. Full of a sense of the peace and stillness of the incomprehensible mysteries of Christianity, the line is also alert with a sense of threat and menace.

'The Holy Innocents' is typical of Lowell's early poetry in that it

2 See Hugh B. Staples, *Robert Lowell: The First Twenty Years*, London 1967, p. 96.
3 See Patrick Cosgrave, *The Public Poetry of Robert Lowell*, London 1970, 1970, pp. 66-75.
4 Ibid., p. 72.

is a poem sharply critical of the world and its values. It juxtaposes the mysteries of belief in redemption with the felt burden of this world and its values ('the world out-Herods Herod; and the year, / The nineteenth-hundred forty-fifth of grace / Lumbers with losses up the clinkered hill / of our purgation'). Unlike many of Lowell's early poems it manages to fuse these opposed senses, so that a feeling of the awe and the peace of the mysteries of faith is communicated.

The three 'Black Rock' poems—'Colloquy in Black Rock', 'Christmas in Black Rock' and 'New Year's Day'—will probably be more clearly understood in the light of later biographical information about Lowell; but while such knowledge will presumably illuminate obscurities, it will not be able to save them from the charge of containing untransformed lumps of feeling and unassimilated conglomerate. Hugh Staples informs us that Lowell lived in Black Rock for some time after his release from Federal Prison in the spring of 1944, that it has a large Hungarian population who worship at St Stephen's, named for the patron saint of Hungary, and overlooks the beach mud flats used as a municipal dump, and the huge Sikorsky helicopter plant. On the Sunday following Corpus Christi Day the feast is celebrated by a special procession and mass, and the 'drumbeat of St Stephen's choir' is taken to refer to the religious parade on 11 June 1944.[5]

The poem is a traditional dialogue of the poet and his soul; the urgent, monotonously relentless rhythm enacts the violent conflict and disturbance within as the poem struggles through a sense of mechanical noise and enveloping mud to reach some vision of God's purpose and presence acting within and above the conflicts of the self and the world. The poem is a celebration for Corpus Christi Day. The opening stanza introduces the idea of inner conflict with the movement from manic violence to depressed stagnation ('All discussions / End in low water, slump and dumps and death'). There is an effort to move beyond the feeling of the conflict and the destruction and the decay of the material to understand more closely the infusion of the spiritual through an awareness of Christ's presence.

> Christ walks on the black water. In Black Mud
> Darts the Kingfisher. On Corpus Christi, heart,
> Over the drum-beat of St Stephen's choir
> I hear him, *Stupor Mundi*, and the mud
> Flies from his hunching wings and beak—my heart,
> The blue kingfisher dives on you in fire.

[5] Staples, *Robert Lowell*, p. 42.

The dissolution of the merely physical leads to a greater sense of the spiritual; Black Rock is broken down into black mud with a vision of the transcendent Christ as the blue kingfisher diving to claim the poet's heart. The movement of the poem is from clenched tension to ecstatic release, and the sense of seeking new bearings is enacted by the clamped patterns of rhyme and rhythm.

'Colloquy in Black Rock' is an extraordinary virtuoso poem and while it has received a considerable amount of exegesis, no one as far as I know has commented on its characteristically brilliant use of assonance and alliterative effects. One or two of these effects are perhaps over-obtrusive and they are certainly virtuoso, but they are justified by their total impact. The whole poem is an address to the heart and the extraordinarily sustained pattern of u sounds (and long a sounds) throughout the whole poem sets up a sense of pulsation, of the heart beating: l.2 (heart), l.3 blood, percussions, l.4 stunned, l.6 discussions, l.7 slump, dump, l.8 mud, l.9 Hungarian, blood, l.10 (martyr), l.11 mud, conjure, mud, l.12 gutted, crust, l.13 mud (harbour) mud, l.14 mud (armoured) tubs, thud, l.15 rust, l.17 trumpet, l.18 (heart) (faster) (faster) mud, l.19 (martyr) blood, l.20 rubbish, l.21 mud, l.22 (darts) (heart), l.23 drum, l.24 mud, l.25 hunching, heart.

It is interesting to note that the last line picks up the i sound from 'flies' in the second last line, again enacting the meaning of the line—the release from, the shaking off of the mud. It is also important to notice the function of the rhyme scheme, where we find repetition rather than rhyme—for instance in stanza two— death, mud, blood, death; in stanza four death, mud, blood, death; stanza five mud, heart, choir, mud, heart, fire. Certainly this is rigid and gives a very forceful sense of being held down, but clearly this effect is intentional and contributes to the meaning of the whole.

'Christmas in Black Rock' and 'New Year's Day' must I think be counted among Lowell's failures. 'Christmas in Black Rock', like 'Colloquy in Black Rock', attempts to use industrial imagery but attains no sense of organic unity as a whole. 'New Year's Day' introduces the image of the suffering and vulnerability of animals which is of major importance throughout Lowell's work. Throughout Lowell's early poems one has, generally speaking, the impression of memorable bits, jewels in a molten setting rather than the sense of fully worked out or organically conceived and shaped wholes. This impression is partly the result of the fact that many of the early poems ('At the Indian Killer's Grave', for instance) have been heavily rewritten, fragments from other poems having been taken over and reassembled, but it also stems from a deeper cause, first noted by R. P. Blackmur, who wrote in his 1945 review of *Land of Unlikeness*:

> Lowell's verse is a beautiful case of citation in any argument in support of the belief in the formal inextricability of the various elements of poetry: meter is not master by itself, any more than attitude or anecdote or perception, though any one of them can be practised by itself at the expense of others, when the tensions become mere fanaticism of spirit and of form: conditions, one would suppose, mutually mutilating. Something of that sort seems to be happening in Lowell's verse. It is as if he demanded *to know* (to judge, to master) both the substance apart from the form with which he handles it and the form apart from the substance handled in order to set them fighting . . . Lowell is distraught about religion; he does not seem to have decided whether his Roman Catholic belief is the form of a force or the sentiment of a form. The result seems to be that in dealing with men his faith compels him to be fractiously vindicitive, and in dealing with faith his experience of men compels him to be nearly blasphemous . . . in Lowell's *Land of Unlikeness* there is nothing loved unless it be its repellence; and there is not a loving meter in the book. What is thought of as Boston in him fights with what is thought of as Catholic; and the fight produces not a tension but a gritting. It is not the violence, the rage, the denial of this world that grits, but the failure of these to find *in verse* a tension of necessity; necessity has, when recognised, the quality of conflict accepted, not hated.[6]

These remarks are particularly relevant to the Black Rock poems and though they are of necessity overstated they do point to that element of rhetorical assertiveness which is so damaging in much of Lowell's early work.

Among the early poems 'The Quaker Graveyard in Nantucket' is the most widely admired, and while sharing some of the qualities (and defects) of other poems of this period, it has an ambition and a scope greater than any other.

'The Quaker Graveyard in Nantucket' is perhaps the most famous of all Lowell's poems. It appeared in *Lord Weary's Castle* in 1946, having been written when Lowell was twenty-eight. The poem's inscription 'For Warren Winslow, Dead at Sea' indicates that first of all it is an elegy, a poem expressing a sense of personal loss for a loved relative. The epigraph—'let man have dominion over the fishes of the sea and the fowls of the air and the beasts and the whole earth, and every creeping creature that moveth upon the earth'—relates to the poem as criticism. It is one of the paradoxes of this piece that while it is a lament for the dead—the

6 Reprinted from his volume *Language as Gesture* copyright 1945 by Richard P. Blackmur).

innocent dead killed in war time—it is also a savage denunciation of the modern world of war and the past America of materialism and greed. A satire on mankind, the poem expresses a sense of *contemptus mundi*. All these different elements—the elegiac, the critical, the prophetic and denunciatory are bound together in the poem through a series of contrasts and juxtapositions that work to interrelate the different levels of meaning and frames of reference. But as well as being these things, 'The Quaker Graveyard' is a poem about the sea, full of a sense of the sights and the sounds, the depths and surfaces, the concrete particulars of the sea itself. This sense of the actual sea merges into the sense of the sea as a symbol. The sea of life is also the sea of death, and the sea in which Warren Winslow and countless others are buried is also the sea from which 'the lord God formed man'. (It is worth noting that nearly every poem that Lowell has written is concerned in one way or another with death and destruction.)

The poem is divided into seven parts of unequal length and begins with the description of the drowned sailor—Warren Winslow—whose body is picked up by a naval vessel:

> The corpse was bloodless, a botch of reds and whites,
> Its open, staring eyes
> Were lustreless dead-lights
> Or cabin-windows on a stranded hulk
> Heavy with sand.

The remains are buried at sea ('where the heel-headed dogfish barks its nose / On Ahab's void and forehead') and the mention of Ahab introduces the references to Melville's *Moby Dick* and the Nantucket Whalers which move through the whole poem. Part I concludes with an acknowledgement of the power of the sea, and a statement, traditional to elegies, that when the time comes for personal death there can be no return from the underworld:

> . . . ask for no Orphean lute
> To pluck life back. The guns of the steeled fleet
> Recoil and then repeat
> The hoarse salute.

The short lines with their sombre sounds, the clipped brevity of the monosyllables suggest both the firing of the guns and the finality of death itself. There can be no return, and poetry cannot pluck life back from the underworld. It is significant that 'lute' is played off against and blocked out by the harsher rhyme word 'salute'; it conveys a bracing vigorous sense of the unsparing facts of life from which there can be no escape in this world. This section introduces two main themes which move through the whole poem: the return of the dead body to the sea ('We weight the body, close / Its eyes and heave it seaward whence it came') —the death of one sailor in war is linked to similar deaths throughout history— and the sense of judgement where man must face the consequences of violence.

It is important to notice from the beginning that the sea itself is associated with violence and death; that the association of death is made directly and explicitly with the sea rather than with a particular aspect of man's nature, cruelty. Death is shown to have dominion throughout, it is like a deity who is all powerful over the strongest man-made resistance (dreadnought):

> Sailors, who pitch this portent at the sea
> Where dreadnoughts shall confess
> Its hell-bent deity,
> When you are powerless
> To sand-bag this Atlantic bulwark, faced
> By the earth-shaker, green, unwearied, chaste.

Death, in fact, equals violence, disfigurement, dissolution symbolized by the sea; and it is interesting to note that all the associations of violence and cruelty are with death itself rather than with man as the inflictor of death. Death is the final and irrevocable fact.

In Part II Lowell uses all the verbal resources of his art to suggest the physical presence of a storm. The violence of the sea is suggested through words like 'heave', 'beating', 'fall', 'break', 'entangled', 'screeching', 'scream', 'wring' and 'cry', while the interplay of plosives and sibilants suggests the various clashing forces of the storm—the bell-buoys and boats resisting the pressure of the sibilants—the forces of the sea—that threaten to undermine them and destroy them.[7] A storm and the death of a cousin in wartime are related to the American past, represented by the Quaker whalers buried in the cemetery, whose destruction of the whales is used to symbolize materialism and greed.

This section primarily aims to express the sense of the terror of death whenever life's calm is disturbed:

> Whenever winds are moving and their breath
> Heaves at the roped-in bulwarks of this pier,
> The terns and sea-gulls tremble at your death

There is repeated reference to insecure bulwarks, sandbags, walls, all those fragile attempts which man makes to fortify himself

---

[7] See Ian Hamilton (ed.), *The Modern Poet*, London 1968, pp. 35-6 for a penetrating observation on this aspect of the poem.

against the surrounding and encroaching element of the sea (which is also the symbol of death). It is interesting to note that the next death image—that of the Quaker Graveyard which is situated at the edge of the land and the sea—is associated with a way of life especially exposed to the sea. The whalers symbolize material greed and through their involvement with worldly gains they are exposed to death as dissolution without transcendence.

In Section III (addressed directly to his cousin) we see the full significance of the poem's epigraph from Genesis. The Quakers of the past had taken the lines 'Let man have dominion over the fishes of the sea' as a justification for their materialism and their ruthless exploitation of nature. Their dreams of success, 'their castles in Spain' are now lost in the seas of time: it is one of life's ironies that they too were destroyed as they destroyed. They died

> When time was open-eyed,
> Wooden and childish; only bones abide
> There, in the nowhere, where their boats were tossed
> Sky-high. . . .

Everything is in 'the hand of the great God'. When he thinks of the Quakers and their pursuit of money, Lowell says:

> What it cost
> Them is their secret. In the sperm-whale's slick
> I see the Quakers drown and hear their cry:
> "If God himself had not been on our side,
> If God himself had not been on our side,
> When the Atlantic rose against us, why,
> Then it had swallowed us up quick."

The Quakers were convinced that God was on their side because he made them so immediately successful; success equalled justification; ends means. The repetition of 'If God himself had not been on our side', adapted from Psalm 124, suggests not only their smugness but also perhaps a need to convince themselves and others through sheer repetition and assertion.

The theme of the vanity of worldly acquisitions and ambitions introduced in Part II is applied to the cousin—the wartime sailor—

> All you recovered from Poseidon died
> With you, my cousin

as well as to the Quakers:

> Whatever it was these Quaker sailors lost
> In the mad scramble of their lives.

In this section the life associated with the sea—the scramble—reveals restlessness, dynamism, flux. Words like 'harrowed' and 'fruitless' suggest sterile activity; while the lines themselves enact a sense of pitching back and forth—'about a waterclock / Of bilge and backwash, roil the salt and sand / Lashing earth's scaffold, rock. . . . '. The use of 'rock' is here almost a trick effect as it momentarily arrests our attention. Rock suggests stability (a cliff), but also instability (movement) and when the word first occurs it is not clear whether it is a noun or a verb until we read on to the next line. The poet's attitude to the Quakers is particularly clear; he views them ironically, but they are used inclusively as an example of the vanity of human wishes and the frailty of human life. They become a universal symbol.

Part IV develops further the central graveyard image. The Quakers are lured on by greed for fortune and their life of vanity and insecurity is indicated through references to 'snatching at straws to sail / Seaward and seaward on the turntail whale'. The whalers and whales, hunter and prey all disappear without trace, blotted out by tides.

> This is the end of running on the waves;
> We are poured out like water.

The instability and impermanence of this life are further underlined by the reference to the Quakers in their *unstoned* graves. The whole section conveys the sense of being swallowed up by the sea (swell, troubled waters, whirlpools) and the initial violence gives way to the sea-music of the relentless and restless activity of the tides.

Part IV is the most incantatory section of the whole; it is both a lament for the fact of death and a *memento mori*, a reminder of its ineluctability. 'This is the end' is repeated three times and the section finishes with a question about the resurrection 'Who will dance / The mast-lashed master of Leviathans / Up from this field of Quakers in their unstoned graves?' As Terry Miller first pointed out[8], 'The mast-lashed master of Leviathans' is a metaphorical cluster characteristic of Lowell. It recalls

> both Ahab, who was caught up in his own harpoon line and tied to Moby Dick, and the weather look-outs in the masts of the sinking *Pequod*. It also suggests Ulysses, lashed to the mast to avoid being destroyed by the sirens' song. And finally, it brings to mind the image of Christ on the Cross.

Furthermore, one might add, the sense of being helpless and abandoned by God at a time of trial is suggested by reference to the line

---

8 'The Prosodies of Robert Lowell', *Speech Monographs*, XXV, November 1968, p. 429.

from David's Psalm (22:14) 'We are poured out like water', a psalm which begins: 'My God, my God, why hast thou forsaken me?', words later spoken by the crucified Christ.

The poem tends to have a circular questioning pattern, rather than a narrative, linear, chronological sequence, though its whole movement is towards a central resolution of the questions it is concerned with, and this section in particular moves towards the destruction of the Quakers.

In Part V Lowell takes the image of the smell of a whale's rotting entrails to suggest the corruption of a world given to the pursuit of material gains. This spreading evil will have to be accounted for on Judgement Day. There is a sense not only of the violation of nature and the natural order but also of transgressions against the holy and sacred: 'The death-lance churns into the sanctuary'. This apocalyptic section suggests the violence and cruelty inflicted and to be suffered by man and seems to refer not only to what the Quakers did to the whales but to the torments of damnation. The section moves rapidly from a fiercely evocative description of the killing of a whale (based largely and closely on Chapter LXI, 'Stubb Kills A Whale' in *Moby Dick*)[9] to the death of Christ: the lance that plunges into the whale is compared with the spear that pierced Christ's side. 'Hide, / Our steel, Jonas Messias, in Thy side'. Miller has further commented on the ambiguity of these lines:

> The name, Jonas Messias, linked Jonah, who learned of God's power through being swallowed by a whale, with Christ. Both of these men are also linked with the whale itself. The 'steel', then, is both a harpoon, and the spear that pierced Christ's side. The complexity is enhanced through the punctuaticn of the line. If the line were meant simply as a plea to Jonas Messias, it would read 'Hide / Our steel . . .' with no comma. The presence of the comma makes the line an address to the steel as well as to the whale-deity. If the line is a prayer, it is also the harpooner's heathen command for his harpoon to fly true.[10]

This seems to me an important observation. However, the line also prepares us for the next explicitly religious section in its recognition of the need for forgiveness and other-worldly interventions.

Part VI, with its special heading, 'Our Lady of Walsingham',[11]

9 Cf. Jerome Mazzaro, *The Poetic Themes of Robert Lowell*, Michigan 1965, p. 40.
10 'The Prosodies of Robert Lowell', p. 429.
11 The reference is to the shrine at the Carmelite Monastery of Walsingham in Norfolk, England, the most popular shrine to Mary in pre-Reformation days until it was destroyed in the year 1538. (See De Sales Standerwick: 'Notes on

marks an abrupt change of tone in the whole work and provides the utmost contrast to the preceding apocalyptic section. So far the poem has been one of almost unrelieved violence and savagery—a poem about war, storms, death and the killing of whales. The violent presence of storms and war has been related to the cruelty and competitive ruthlessness of the past; contempt for the violence and destructiveness of the present. The situations have been presented and juxtaposed, the parallels drawn. Part VI tries to offer some resolution of the dilemma; it is a vision of salvation. Our Lady represents the religious peace and certainty of the past and is used to suggest an other-worldly solution to this world of conflict, destruction and greed. We are told she knows something of 'what God knows / Not Calvary's Cross nor crib at Bethlehem'. 'Expressionless, expresses God'. She represents then 'the peace that passeth understanding', that transcends the conflicts we cannot solve, and is asked as she was asked by the pilgrims at her shrine to intercede on behalf of man who cannot fathom the incomprehensible power of God. This section is full of a sense of harmony and tranquillity: 'Now, and the world shall come to Walsingham'. The setting is inland and rural as opposed to the sea of the other sections; the image is peaceful and miniaturistic as opposed to the violent and gigantic, suggesting the timeless where the other sections are concerned with death, flux and the life in time. There is too a remarkable sense of slowness in this section; a feeling of the static as opposed to the extraordinary dynamism of earlier sections.

> There once the penitents took off their shoes
> And then walked barefoot the remaining mile;
> And the small trees, a stream and hedgerows file
> Slowly along the munching English lane,
> Like cows to the old shrine, until you lose
> Track of your dragging pain.
> The stream flows down under the druid tree,
> Shiloah's whirlpools gurgle and make glad
> The castle of God. Sailor, you were glad
> And whistled Sion by that stream.

Section VII returns us once again to the dominating images of the sea; it is a seascape after the salvation vision. There is a sense of spent calm after the storm, but it is not Utopian or transcendent.

Robert Lowell', *Renascence*, VIII, 1955-6, p. 77. Jerome Mazzaro, pp. 41-2, and Hugh B. Staples, pp. 103-4, give the relevant extracts from Edward I. Watkin's *Catholic Art and Culture* (New York, 1944) which describe this statue of the 'Queen of Contemplatives'. Lowell himself of course first drew attention to this source in a prefatory note to *Lord Weary's Castle*.

The sea is full of corpses, foulness and dissolution; and there is the sense of having come full circle as the brackish winds echo the 'brackish shoal' of the opening of the poem. The section returns to the images of the past. The great 'wing'd clippers' of the whaling days are recalled; as the storm begins to subside and settle, the atmospheric awareness of the sea makes Lowell recall the origin of life itself when 'The Lord God formed man from the sea's slime'. The calm referred to here is stagnant, quite unlike the calm of Section VI; but in the slime and rot of death there is a recollection of the creation of life. The implication seems to be not so much hope for regeneration and new life out of death, though perhaps this exists, as the almost inevitable exposure to death which goes with the gift of life:

> When the Lord God formed man from the sea's slime
> And breathed into his face the breath of life,
> And blue-lung'd combers lumbered to the kill.

Yet God survives the apparent paradox and insolubility of this double gift, and the poem ends with an affirmation of faith and an assertion that God endures behind all the contradictions and manifestations of His power:

> The Lord survives the rainbow of His will.

The last line is curiously ambiguous. If it suggests renewal, new hope for man, De Sales Standerwick is surely right to detect an ominous note in it as well:

> The Book of Genesis relates how God made a covenant with Noah after the destructive flood: 'I will set my bow in the clouds, and it shall be the sign of a convenant between me, and between the earth.' The rainbow is the sign of hope and salvation; but if we do not fulfil our part of the covenant, the Lord will 'render to every man according to his deeds.' Thus the poem ends on a dire note with the threat that Ahab's fate may be our own if the monster overtakes us.[12]

There is much in Lowell's early work that is strained, over-intense and rhetorical, and even a poem like 'The Quaker Grave-yard' can seem more brilliant than moving. It is a poem of considerable rhetorical energy, its verbal violence and force being appropriate to its theme of present and past destruction. But one's response to its religious message will depend on one's previous convictions rather than on anything the poem does. The poem works through juxtapositions, and the movement from Section V to Section VI is an abrupt cut in tone, a sudden shift of emphasis

12 'Notes on Robert Lowell', p. 78.

which juxtaposes this world with other worldly values. The world of horror and violence is so well conveyed that the abrupt change to the world of religious peace which is Lowell's answer to the hypocrisies, greed and pride of the past, can only seem externally imposed and willed. After what has gone before the tone of 'all shall be well and all manner of things shall be well' is likely to strike one as a little bland; and while the last two sections ostensibly 'resolve' the issues of the poem there is a noticeable diminution in their poetic power.

'The Quaker Graveyard in Nantucket' is a traditional elegy and its affiliations with other great elegies—Milton's 'Lycidas', Shelley's 'Adonais' and Hopkins' 'The Wreck of the Deutschland'—have been noted by critics and commentators from the time of its first appearance. On the level of ideas and structure, in its mingling of Christian and pagan symbolism and its interweaving of criticism of aspects of the world and of human behaviour, it resembles these other great elegies. Lowell is a highly literate poet, using all the traditional resources of English poetry that he can muster and master; behind most of his early poems are literary models many veiled literary allusions, compacted borrowings, implicit or explicit literary references. The study of these in any detail would require a separate book, but aspects of the work have already been undertaken. Hugh Staples has shown, for instance, something of the use Lowell has made in 'The Quaker Graveyard' of borrowings from Thoreau's *Cape Cod*, Melville's *Moby Dick*, and E. I. Watkin's *Catholic Art and Culture* in the Our Lady of Walsingham section; and I shall treat in some detail the use of allusions in *Life Studies*. This all points to Lowell's highly concentrated literary training; he started writing in the formalist 'forties when a high degree of formalism and multiple literary cross-referencing were a feature of much of the poetry. But at its best it serves a highly functional purpose, as in the borrowing of Donne's stanza form from 'A Nocturnal upon St Lucy's Day' as the framework for 'Mr Edwards and the Spider': here the stanza-form is used to express an argument which in itself characterizes the ideas and the mind of the speaker.

In many of his early poems Lowell uses aspects of the interior monologue to reveal character and surroundings. He has always needed strong, objective and elaborate forms to engage his mind and discipline his imagination. Lowell once planned to write a biography of Jonathan Edwards (1703-58), the greatest of the American puritan divines. He is a figure referred to in several other poems ('After The Surprising Conversions' in *Poems 1938-1949*; 'Jonathan Edwards in Western Massachusetts' in *For The*

Union Dead; 'The Worst Sinner' in *Notebook*) and a figure central to Lowell's imagination. Jonathan Edwards was a most influential theologian who revived Calvinist doctrines in America. At the age of twenty he underwent a mystical experience which enabled him to accept the Calvinist doctrine of 'unconditional election'. He believed, that is, that God arbitrarily chooses to save a few individuals while the rest are condemned to perdition.

Lowell's poem—it is both a character poem and a monologue—is a direct address by Edwards to his uncle Joseph Hawley who in a state of deep depression cut his throat and died on 1 June 1735. Hawley had been thrown into a state of despair by Edwards' sermons and beliefs, convinced that he could not possibly be one of the saved. The poem draws its phrasing[13] from two of Edwards' most important essays: 'Of Insects' and 'The Future Punishment of the Wicked' in such a way that they become part of Edwards' observation and reflection.

Lowell makes a short, dramatic narrative out of Edwards' discursive prose; the poem begins with the fine description of the spiders marching through the air as they move to their apparently purposeless death in the sea. Edwards immediately postulates an analogy through his question 'What are we in the hands of the great God?' using this piece of natural observation as an image of God's attitude to man. 'We are in the hand of the great God' as helpless as the spider; we are kept alive only by the will of God. Mazzaro and Donoghue in particular have shown how Lowell is here using lines from Edwards' sermon 'Sinners in the Hands of An Angry God'.

> You hang by a slender thread, with the flames of divine wrath flashing it, and ready every moment to singe it and burn it asunder; and you have no interest in any Mediator and nothing to lay hold of to save yourself, nothing to keep off the flames of wrath, nothing of your own, nothing that you have ever done, nothing that you can do, to induce God to spare you one moment.

Lowell writes:

> A very little thing, a little worm,
> Or hourglass-blazoned spider, it is said,
> Can kill a tiger. Will the dead
> Hold up his mirror and affirm
> To the four winds the smell
> And flash of his authority? It's well
> If God who holds you to the pit of hell,

13 See Dennis Donoghue, *Connoisseurs of Chaos*, London 1965, pp. 154-7, Mazzaro, *The Poetic Themes*, pp. 66-71, and Staples, *Robert Lowell*, pp. 98-9.

> Much as one holds a spider, will destroy,
>   Baffle and dissipate your soul. . . .

The smallest thing can kill a tiger, but God the tiger is all power-
ful and nothing human can assert its force or authority against
him 'who holds you to the pit of hell'.

In the last two stanzas Edwards recollects that as a small boy he
saw a spider die when it was thrown into a fire and how, once in
the fire it could not move or escape; it had no will of its own. The
spider is compared with the damned soul or the soul of a person
who has been refused salvation, and by a clever concentration and
intensification of the image, death and damnation are seen as one:

> But who can plumb the sinking of that soul?
> Josiah Hawley, picture yourself cast
>   Into a brick-kiln where the blast
>   Fans your quick vitals to a coal—
>   If measured by a glass,
> How long would it seem burning! Let there pass
> A minute, ten, ten trillion; but the blaze
> Is infinite, eternal: this is death,
> To die and know it. This is the Black Widow, death.

In making Edwards address Josiah Hawley directly, Lowell indi-
vidualizes and thus intensifies the poem's almost hysterical obses-
sion with damnation, time, death and the realities of Hell. Some
readers see the poem as an ironical portrait of Edwards and his
extreme views; but this is a reading that is hard if not impossible
to justify from the text itself. Geoffrey Hill has commented more
perceptively on the imaginative disposition of the material, which
'releases both the tone of magisterial dogmatism and the note of
childish exaggeration and causes them to interact'.[14] The poem's
achievement is, I think, twofold; first to present a portrait of the
intensities of Edwards' obsessions—of his Calvinist god—and then,
through a slight shift in the weight of the image, to move the
emphasis from a concern with damnation to a deeply-felt fear of
death and dying and the progressively heightened sense of human
insignificance in front of the cessation of consciousness. So, to put
it oversimply, fear of Hell merges with fear of death, of the know-
ledge of death and becomes inseparable from it. Like 'The Quaker
Graveyard' the poem shows the inexplicable majesty of God, his
terrible power, and points to the helplessness of the human con-
dition.

Some of Lowell's poems fail through the unexpected suddenness

14 *Essays in Criticism*, XIII, 1963, p. 192.

of their transitions or through their abrupt changes in mood. 'The First Sunday in Lent', for instance, begins with a remarkable sense of atmosphere and a sharp rendering of the poet's sense of isolation in the family attic:

> This is the fifth floor attic where I hid
> My stolen agates and the cannister
> Preserved from Bunker Hill—feathers and guns,
> Matchlock and flintlock and percussion-cap;
> Gettysburg etched upon the cylinder
> Of Father's Colt. A Luger of a Hun,
> Once blue as Satan, breaks Napoleon,
> My china pitcher. Cartridge boxes trap
> A chipmunk on the sabre where they slid.

This is a fine evocation of his childhood's world of fascination with guns and soldiers and military equipment, but the poem then moves to a reference to Troy's last day:

> On Troy's last day, alas, the populous
> Shrines held carnival, and girls and boys
> Flung garlands to the wooden horse; so we
> Burrow into the lion's mouth to die.
> Lord, from the lust and dust thy will destroys
> Raise an unblemished Adam who will see
> The limbs of the tormented chestnut tree
> Tingle, and hear the March-winds lift and cry:
> 'The Lord of Hosts will overshadow us.'

It is a plea for release from the powers that rule this world. The poet is initially looking down on the cold beginning of Lent and, as he sees the crowds below, prays for release into a new life, a new world. He prays to the Lord to 'raise an unblemished Adam' and to give protection.

The second part of this poem 'The Ferris Wheel' takes an old image—the wheel of fortune—and uses it allegorically as an image of the world of Vanity Fair. The world of danger and imminent destruction is compared with the world of the circus where the trickster Satan is in command.

'Christmas Eve Under Hooker's Statue' is one of Lowell's exhortatory poems. A bitter condemnation of war, the poem is set at night in a blackout and again merges recollections from the innocence of childhood with the world of modern war and materialism. It is Christmas during a time of war and nothing could throw into sharper relief the conflicts raging in the modern world than this traditional time of the birth of peace. The speaker of the poem is standing near a statue of Joseph Hooker, the Civil

31

War general who commanded the Union Army in its defeat at Chancellorsville, and a sense of the futility of war in the past and in the present is expressed throughout. In the first stanza the emphasis falls on the bitterness of knowing and of knowledge: the child loses innocence, ideals are destroyed in war; innocence and hope are defeated in the modern world ('I ask for bread, my father gives me mould'). Images of Christmas as a time for presents from Santa Claus and a time of peace and the birth of Christ are interrelated with the sense of innocence and childishness, knowledge and bitter awareness.

> When Chancellorsville mowed down the volunteer,
> "All wars are boyish," Herman Melville said;
> But we are old, our fields are running wild:
> Till Christ again turn wanderer and child.

Although the poem ends with an appeal to Christian belief to relieve the misery and horror of the modern world and to offer a value which transcends the mingling of good and evil in this world, the weight of the poem falls more heavily on the sense of the corruption and disorder of the modern world. As Richard Fein says

> Though the poem at the end considers a way of emerging from the holocaust, it never convinces us that the resurrection of the spirit is possible, only that it is desirable.[15]

The family poems in *Poems 1938-1949* are among the best and most accessible of these pieces. 'Buttercups', according to Staples, was originally published as Part 2 of 'Passages from "The Quaker Graveyard"' which appeared in the *Partisan Review*, XIII (Winter 1946).[16] A series of memories of childhood with his cousin, this small poem is one of the most perfect in the collection. Lowell recalls moments from childhood and childish games, but how 'there were shod hoofs behind the horseplay'.

> I played Napoleon in my attic cell
> Until my shouldered broom
> Bobbed down the room
> With horse and neighing shell.

The poem shows with a heavily restrained pathos (the movement of the lines seems to suggest some sense of contained and then overflowing grief) that there is no escape from cruelty and violence either in life or in the imagination. The attic seems to offer a place

---

15 Richard J. Fein, *Robert Lowell*, New York 1970, pp. 25, 26.
16 Staples, *Robert Lowell*, p. 90.

of withdrawal but there the huge print of Waterloo also reminds him of aspects of life's destructiveness:

> I cried
> To see the Emperor's sabred eagle slide
> From the clutching grenadier
> Staff-Officer
> With the gold leaf cascading down his side—
> A red dragoon, his plough-horse rearing, swayed
> Back on his reins to crop
> The buttercup
> Bursting upon the braid.

Nothing could express more poignantly the sense of life's fragility than the final image of the buttercup 'bursting upon the braid'.

This is an extraordinarily evocative poem, charged with feeling without using any directly emotive words. The cruelty of life, the destruction of youthful heroism, the sense of frail nobility are frequent themes in Robert Lowell. This poem is in some ways a foreshadowing of 'For the Union Dead' or of the image of Colonel Robert Shaw: all youthful idealism is contained in the image of the young officer. Here (and in this 'Buttercups' differs from many of the other war poems) we are not presented with an image of random destruction by senseless war, but with a sense of the inevitable destruction of youthful ideals and nobility by brute force— in the unmounted officer (there is at least no mention of his horse) at the mercy of the dragoon on the plough-horse.

The process of the poem is to show the impossibility of escape, the impingement of reality upon every refuge. The first image is of the security of childhood with its sense of the solid parental buttress ('our papas were stout'), but already there is lack of identity and stability ('And colourless as seaweed on the floats'). The second sentence suggests the secure, isolated world of childhood ('We were shut / In gardens'), but the cruelty and destructiveness of reality are latent in the childish games themselves and do not need to come from without. One notes the effectiveness and menace of 'There were shod hoofs behind the horseplay' which develops the literal meaning of part of the phrase through the slight but controlled pathos of 'thin [opposed to the stout papas] / And up-turned chin' (with its suggestions of vulnerability and frail pride). The third line of defence is the 'attic cell', something of a fantasy world in which he identifies himself with the Napoleonic officer. This world is dominated by historical reality as depicted by the print and more shattering in its impact than personally suffered injuries: 'I played Napoleon' and 'I cried to see . . .' The juxtaposition of the 'smile' of the picture—its 'cracked smile across the glass', with the breaking into tears of the child suggests the triumphant mockery of an adversary who is established at the very centre of the child's refuge. The strong emotional impact of this poem coupled with its apparent simplicity seems to justify a close look at the patterns within the poem. There is certainly no suggesting that all of these are calculated, but analysis can reveal patterns instinctively or organically created. Even where this seems far-fetched, it is pointing to something which, perhaps without obvious significance in itself, helps to set up a sense of relationships and therefore of coherence and significance in the poem as a whole.

It is worth noting that in this poem there are (for Lowell) relatively few sound effects or patterns; most of the effect comes through images and rhythm. The recurrent images which unify and relate the parts of the poem are flowers in stanzas one and two (black-eyed susan and buttercup) and the image of the horse: shod hoofs, horseplay, horse, neighing shell, plough-horse rearing. The other unifying effect comes from words suggesting swaying movement: floats, bending out into the ocean, bobbed, slide and swayed. The rhythm and the use of short lines and long lines also contributes to this sense of movement as well as serving to focus on specific images: staff officer, the buttercup and the braid. It would be wrong, I think, to plot some specific significance to any of these images; they are used in the way a painter deploys patches of colour, not simply to refer to a reality, but to set up a pattern, a system of relationships which exists only in the picture and gives it impact and coherence. (Cf. also my comments later on bird images in 'Falling Asleep Over the Aeneid').

It is also interesting to note the use of colours in 'Buttercups'. In stanza one no colours are mentioned, but the word 'colourless' occurs early; then only 'brassy' and 'black' are mentioned, no real colours, whereas in stanza two the scene of the picture comes to more vivid life than childhood's reality; blue, gold, red and buttercup are mentioned with a strong evocation of clear colour. The use of the central buttercup image then is especially effective. All the associations of youthful freshness, simplicity, beauty and a certain natural vigour can be suggested without obvious pathos or any dimming of one's sense of the concrete.

Even in his early elegies like 'In Memory of Arthur Winslow', Lowell is concerned to question and reject the Puritan tradition of his New England forbears, the Winslows. In the early elegies there is a questioning of the Calvinist idea of predestination, of the dividing of the world into the elect and the damned.

34

'In Memory of Arthur Winslow' is divided into four parts, 'Death from Cancer', 'Dunbarton', 'Five Years Later' and 'A Prayer for My Grandfather to Our Lady' closely grouped to show the nature of Winslow's destiny and the destiny of the tradition he represents.

In Part I, 'Death from Cancer' Lowell addresses his ancestor who is dying of cancer and tells him that he will only live until Death comes to crush the crab. It is Easter, but the noise of the holiday makers 'dwarfs' the ringing of the Easter bells. In the second stanza he addresses his grandfather thus:

> Grandfather Winslow, look, the swanboats coast
> That island in the Public Gardens, where
> The bread-stuffed ducks are brooding, where with tub
> And strainer the mid-Sunday Irish scare
> The sun-struck shallows for the dusky chub
> This Easter, and the ghost
> Of risen Jesus walks the waves to run
> Arthur upon a trumpeting black swan
> Beyond Charles River to the Acheron
> Where the wide waters and their voyager are one.

He wants to suggest the entrance of the dead man into the world of oblivion which is also the world of heaven and salvation for the believing Christian. The stately movement of the last lines with their rich expansiveness suggest the peaceful and total absorption of the dead man into the world of death.

'Dunbarton' is a poem about the burial of Arthur Winslow. The opening stanza with its ten run-on, unpunctuated lines has a flat insistence, a disenchanted sharpness of observation: the stones are yellow, the grass grey, the lake rotten. It is about the death of a tradition represented both by the very old—the half crippled, the half deaf—present at the grandfather's funeral ('half-forgotten Starks and Winslows fill / The granite plot') and the fact of the unfulfilment of the tradition they represented: 'O fearful witnesses, your day is done.' The second stanza emphasizes the perfunctoriness of the burial rites and their essential emptiness ('The minister from Boston waves your shades, / Like children, out of sight and out of mind').

Part III 'Five Years Later' is the most overtly critical section of the poem. Lowell, mourning the man, nevertheless condemns his grandfather's materialism and his uncompromising pursuit of material wealth and gain.

> I came to mourn you, not to praise the craft
> That netted you a million dollars, late
> Hosing out gold in Colorado's waste,

Then lost it all in Boston real estate.
Now from the train, at dawn
Leaving Columbus in Ohio, shell
On shell of our stark culture strikes the sun
To fill my head with all our fathers won
When Cotton Mather wrestled with the fiends from hell.

The two stanzas of the poem are linked through the word craft, with its suggestions of craftiness and graft as well as of art and trade. The old Puritan tradition in fact prepared the way for the modern materialism of contemporary American society; but Arthur Winslow's ancestors were also inspired by a sense of family craft and sustained by some sense of public, creative achievement. Edward Winslow (1595-1655), once a governor of Plymouth and one of the Pilgrim Fathers who came over on the *Mayflower* built the block-house at Marshfield; his grandson Edward (1669-1753) was a well-known sheriff and silversmith, while General Stark (1728-1822), the Revolutionary war general founded the township of Dunbarton.[17] Although Arthur Winslow was driven by ambition and greed, Lowell says of him 'You must have hankered for our family's craft'

. . . for what else could bring
You, Arthur, to the veined and alien West
But devil's notions that your gold at least
Could give back life to men who whipped or backed the King?

In other words, there must have been some belief that he could use his money to do good, but Lowell condemns this as more than a mistaken idea—as a devil's notion—in the belief that the making of money is itself an evil.

'A Prayer for my Grandfather to Our Lady' is a prayer by Lowell for intercession on the part of the Virgin Mary to bless and spiritually cleanse and renew the world. In the first four lines he points out how his forbears, with their commercial pursuits ('our clippers' and 'our slavers') never found the 'haven of your peace'— i.e. Roman Catholic belief in the Virgin Mary. In the next seven lines, with a kind of baroque bravura, Lowell begs Mary for her blessing: 'I implore / Your scorched, blue thunderbreasts to pour / Buckets of blessings on my burning head / Until I rise like Lazarus from the dead'. By changing 'me' to 'us' in the quotation from Psalms, 1, 7 (Vulgate)—*Lavabis nos et super nivem dealabor*— Lowell is able to include his grandfather and all his forbears in his prayer.

17 See Mazzaro, *The Poetic Themes*, p. 15 and Marjorie Perloff, 'Death by Water, The Winslow Elegies of Robert Lowell', *ELH*, XXXIV, 1967, p. 121.

In the second stanza, which adapts some lines from Villon's prayer written for his mother to our Lady, Lowell pictures the stained-glass windows in the costly Protestant Trinity Church in Boston to suggest the limits of his grandfather's faith: it was a world where 'hell is burnt out, heaven's harp-strings are slack'. And though the window is meant to depict the triumph of heavenly over materialistic, earthly things with the destruction of the power of Satan, the suggestion is clear that his grandfather's religious beliefs were more this- than other-worldly and lacked the mystical dimension. Thus the significance of the last two lines:

> Mother, run to the chalice, and bring back
> Blood on your finger-tips for Lazarus who was poor.

The two stanzas are held together by a double Biblical allusion both to the Lazarus of Luke XVI, 19-31 as well as to the Lazarus of John XI.[18] The first Lazarus is poor and is not allowed to intercede for 'the certain rich man' in hell; the other Lazarus is a symbol of the Resurrection. The implication of these two references is that Lowell's own intercession may be fruitless but that his grandfather may find salvation and resurrection on the last day. Thus the questioning and criticizing of Winslow materialism and the exposed limitation of its religious piety is transcended in a prayer that suggests the possibility of some kind of other worldly fulfilment and release.

'Winter in Dunbarton' is one of the most curious of the early poems, a strange combination of corruption, filth and rot with coldness. On first reading it seems an oddly fragmented piece, full of an almost incoherent nausea; it is remarkable for being one of the few poems that seem to express revulsion from life as a whole rather than just from some particular aspect of man's behaviour. The images obviously have strong subjective significance, but are not sufficiently moulded to hold the emotional charge projected into them—hence the sense of incoherent fury that seems to characterize the piece as a whole. It is a poem that has never been explicated, but it is, I am convinced, a piece about Time—one of the great themes of modern literature and an obsessive concern in poetry of the late 1930s and 1940s.

Time—to paraphrase for a moment—'smiling on this sundial of a world' is all destroying in 'this eldest of the seasons'. It is necessary to see that cold itself is in the poem an image of time: hence the strange juxtapositions—'the snowman and the worm'. Time

18 See Staples, *Robert Lowell*, p. 98; Mazzaro, *The Poetic Themes*, p. 18; Perloff, 'Death by Water', p. 123; Cosgrave, *The Public Poetry*, p. 62.

(cold) is inimical to man; it is malevolent rather than indifferent: 'a world against our world'; cold destroys both the simple, insignificant animal (cat) and the apparently timeless work of art, more specifically Christian art, which might hope to survive on two counts, as art and as Christian belief. But cold snaps it, breaks it back to the element from which it was shaped. It is worth noting that the images of the bronze-age shards of Christ' and of the cat ('tight as a boulder') are both related to the father: 'Belle, the cat that used to rat / About my father's books' and 'the Christ / My father fetched from Florence'. These are symbols of two extremes encompassed by a human life—that which is tender, trivial and transient ('she no longer hears / Her catnip turtle squeaking') and that which is apparently timeless through the perfection of its form and the significance of its message, as well as through the sheer durability of its material. All are destroyed by time/cold which, further, through them destroys also the memory of the already dead father:

> Cold
> Snaps the bronze toes and fingers of the Christ
> My father fetched from Florence, and the dead
> Chatters to nothing in the thankless ground
> His father screwed from Charlie Stark and sold
> To the selectmen. Cold has cramped his head
> Against his heart: my father's stone is crowned
> With snowflakes and the bronze-age shards of Christ.

Is there some hint of hope in those last lines, in the acceptance of this destruction? The image of the snowflakes as a crown invests transience itself with a regal quality and destruction seems to become timelessness ('the bronze-age shards of Christ'). But this is far from being unambiguous: it is not part of the analysable meaning or is at least only one possibility supported by the movement of the line. There is a long, strong surge, a sense of confidence which comes from the unbroken flow of the line—all the more forceful after the pauses in the previous two lines. It is interesting, too, to note the weight of Christ as the final word in the stanza and in the poem; the same word rhymes with itself. Such a paradoxical effect in the last lines is characteristic of a number of Lowell poems: they seem to be full of hope and are yet ambiguous (like the ending of 'The Quaker Graveyard') or, as at the end of 'Buttercups', a surge of hope is inextricably bound up with an image or movement of destruction.

Among the early family poems, 'Mary Winslow' is one of the most perfectly shaped and achieved. This elegy for Lowell's grandmother, like the poem to his grandfather, combines Christian and pagan and historical references into an image of old and new Boston and the social world represented by the Winslows. References to the Charles River, Charon and the Boston Boat Club are used as in the earlier poem to give resonance and universal significance to an individual death. The poem has a complete unity of texture and tone. Compared with her husband, whose energies were directed towards material gain and worldly pursuits, Mary Winslow is shown as having declined into a childish senility fully in keeping with her original character; we are told 'the body cools / And smiles as a sick child'; there is reference to her hideous baby-squawks and yells and to the childish bibelots that surrounded her, and 'her terrified and child's cold eyes' mirror a John Singleton Copley portrait of an ancestress.

This poem, too, depicts aspects of a family in decline. Now that Mary Winslow is dead nothing will be the same again. Heirlooms and family objects are veiled and put away. As in 'Buttercups' there is a developed image linking the two stanzas of the poem. The image of 'the twinned runt bulls' connects with the image of 'the bestial cow' in the next section (a reference to the fact that cows were allowed to be grazed on Boston Common until the privilege was rescinded after World War II.)[19] It serves to suggest the decline of the old rural way of life fast disappearing under the development of modern urban Boston, an idea developed in several other early poems and present in *Life Studies* and *For the Union Dead*. There is an almost mock-heroic bravura about the poem, the rhetorical swing of the whole giving a touch of solemnity which contrasts effectively and poignantly with the childishness and vulnerability of Mary Winslow herself.

The two sonnets 'Salem' and 'Concord' go together in taking two places of great significance in American history for their titles; both places are associated with New England's mercantile past; both are used as vantage points for scoring off and criticizing New England's past and present; both question the colonial heritage. In 'Salem' the point of departure is a sailor knitting in an old seaman's home and the opening images suggest sleep and death and stagnation. The poem ends:

> Remember, seaman, Salem fishermen
> Once hung their nimble fleets on the Great Banks.
> Where was it that New England bred the men
> Who quartered the Leviathan's fat flanks
> And fought the British Lion to his knees?

19 See John J. McAleer, *The Explicator*, XVIII, February 1960, p. 29.

The rhetorical question here is a jibe at all that Salem might be said to stand for, but the obvious criticism to make is that whatever causes Lowell to propose his judgment of Salem remains obstinately outside the poem.

'Concord' is altogther more successful as a whole, being built on a series of comparisons between the present and the past in a way that shows their interrelationship. 'Ten thousand Fords are idle here in search / Of a tradition' the poem begins, and the sonnet itself searches for the meaning of the tradition which has degenerated. Here as elsewhere Lowell is concerned with one of the paradoxes of American culture as he sees it: the decline of the God-fearing hard-working Puritan Christian faith into the working of 'Mammon's unbridled industry'. It is the paradox of a religious faith that believing in the value of hard work accumulated so much wealth and power in this world that its values became this-worldly and led to its modern capitalist power. It is the problem of the absence of belief in Grace. The last five lines powerfully point to another paradox of New England culture—that behind all the pacifistic and peace-loving activities of a Thoreau, for instance, lie the brutal facts of history, the grim realities of the wars against the indians:

> This Church is Concord—Concord where Thoreau
> Named all the birds without a gun to probe
> Through darkness to the painted man and bow:
> The death-dance of King Philip and his scream
> Whose echo girdled this imperfect globe.

As so often in these early poems Lowell is able to make some effective points through his use of contrasts and juxtapositions, but they often leave a nagging sense of dissatisfaction in the reader's mind. A smiliar sense of disquiet strikes the reader of 'Children of Light':

> Our fathers wrung their bread from stocks and stones
> And here the pivoting searchlights probe to shock
> Embarking from the Nether Land of Holland,
> Pilgrims unhoused by Geneva's night,
> They planted here the Serpent's seeds of light;
> And here the pivoting searchlights probe to shock
> The riotous glass houses built on rock,
> And candles gutter by an empty altar,
> And light is where the landless blood of Cain
> Is burning, burning the unburied grain.

This ten line poem is carefully structured and divided into five line sections, that are related and pivot on the word *here*, the word that links the past and the present. It is an attack by Lowell on his Puritan heritage as he attempts to show a connection between his Calvinist forbears who killed the Indians ('They planted here the Serpent's seeds of light')—a heavily charged ironic line—and the farmers who are now burning their grain. The rather obscure details in lines seven and eight may refer (like some parts of 'The Quaker Graveyard') to modern war, with the light of searchlights catching in the glass of the glasshouses; ('those who live in glasshouses' suggests fragility even if the houses are built on the rock of faith,) the burning of the grain refers to the burning of grain during the Depression.[20] The lines would seem to have a more immediate contemporary reference, making the same connection between past and present that Lowell posits, for instance, in 'The Quaker Graveyard in Nantucket' and 'Christmas Eve Under Hooker's Statue'. What strikes one is the note of contempt Lowell is able to express through the insistently childish rhythm of the opening lines; and there is anger and contempt in the relationship and opposition he posits. But the poem finally works through too simple, too emblematic an opposition to be wholly convincing in the way that—to take one example only—a poem like 'Fall 1961' convinces.

A group of six sonnets form something of a sequence in their combined concern with aspects of man and present violence. 'Napoleon Crosses the Beresina' focuses on Napoleon's disastrous retreat from Russia, again concentrating on images of ice and snow, while 'The Soldier' shows the soldier becoming a mere thing, fighting for and then fought over by two angels with bill-hooks. The next four poems are all violent adaptations from foreign poets: Rimbaud in 'War', Valéry in 'Charles the Fifth and the Peasant', Rilke in 'The Shako' and Villon in 'France'. There seems little point in labouring or lamenting the fact that these poems, like many of Lowell's imitations, are so different in texture and tone and feeling from their originals: Lowell has simply plundered, using the originals as points of departure or as frameworks for his own concerns.

Although a sonnet, 'The North Sea Undertaker's Complaint' does not belong to this group in either subject matter or preoccupation; it merits attention for its own sake and because it is a remarkable poem not usually commented on. It is no less flawed and obscure (in its references and its emotional source) than several

[20] See Fein, *Robert Lowell*, p. 8 and George P. Elliott (ed.), *Fifteen Modern American Poets*, New York 1956, p. 308.

other early poems, but it conveys quite a different sense of power and vigour from the force and detachment of its observed detail. The central image is not fully harnessed to the cerebral issues of the poem, but it does give some sense of weight and dimension to the poem, rather than leaving it just as attitude, opinion or belief. The poem begins with the beautifully observed and rendered flight of the duck:

> Now south and south and south the mallard heads,
> His green-blue bony hood echoes the green
> Flats of the Weser, and the mussel beds
> Are sluggish where the webbed feet spanked the lean
> Eel grass to tinder in the take-off. South
> Is what I think of.

Here the sound effects (like those which evoke the movement of the sea in Section IV of 'The Quaker Graveyard') are not just virtuoso; there is the sense of the lines and the meaning coming alive with the throb of movement. Mazzaro may be right to say that this is intended as a poem about 'the death of religious persons in war time'[21], but in fact it is a poem about the coming of winter ice, the freezing of the river; and the images of death and martyrdom are associated with the season itself. Staples' suggestion[22] that this poem is a piece of genre painting, perhaps even based on a painting, seems closer to the mood of the whole. But the winter ice represents a force that has power to transcend death (the fire of the heart can melt ice), and perhaps even the sense of mystical union which Mazzaro relates to some sentences by St Bernard on the nature of contemplative experience.[23] What, in my view, makes this poem so impressive is the concrete observed detail, evident not only on the level of vocabulary but as a quickening of sound and movement throughout. This sense of quickening is absent in 'Salem', 'Concord', 'Children of Light', 'Rebellion', 'Drunken Fishermen', 'Napoleon Crosses the Beresina' and 'The Soldier'. Most of these pieces seem to be all in the mind, pieces in which ideas generate ideas rather than investing observed reality with significance. (Another striking example of this tendency is stanza two of 'As A Plane Tree By the Water' where ideas are spun out of ideas.) In some of the earlier poems there are passages of observed detail, and sections which communicate a sense of unique experience:

21 Mazzaro, *The Poetic Themes*, p. 43.
22 Staples, *Robert Lowell*, p. 100.
23 Mazzaro p. 44.

Under our windows, on the rotten logs
The moonbeam, bobbing like an apple, snags
The undertow.
                    ('Christmas in Black Rock')

                    In the snow
The kitten heaved its hindlegs, as it fouled,
And died. We bent it in a Christmas box
                    ('New Year's Day')

How dry time screaks in its fat axle-grease.
                    ('The Crucifix')

                    the gulls
Scream from the squelching wharf-piles . . .
                    ('At the Indian Killer's Grave')

The Chapel's sharp-shinned eagle
                    ('Where the Rainbow Ends')

                    by each nose
The aimless waterlines of eyeball's show
Their greenness.
                    ('The Blind Leading the Blind')

But it has to be said that these observations are complete, enclosed,
hard-edge embellishments of the central thesis of the poems: they
are not allowed, like those in 'The North Sea Undertaker's Com-
plaint', to unfold their own shape and inner possibilities of signi-
ficance.

A few remaining poems merit some attention as a group—'To
Peter Taylor on the Feast of the Epiphany', 'As a Plane Tree by
the Water', 'The Dead in Europe' and 'Where the Rainbow Ends'
—though all remain curiously intransigent examples of Lowell's
first manner with some obscure, even impenetrable details. Lowell
is distinctive enough and sure enough as a poet to convince one
that his more puzzling poems will finally yield a meaning; frag-
ments of his most rebarbatively difficult poems have a way of lodg-
ing in the mind; but the fact remains that they have none of that
purely poetic power of the late poems, or of the baffling simplicity
of consummate art.

The four poems mentioned are all on apocalyptic themes. 'To
Peter Taylor on the Feast of the Epiphany' views the world of war,
the modern world heading towards total destruction, the Armaged-
don which can alone redeem it, against the background of the
birth of Christ. The Feast of the Epiphany celebrates the day on

which the Wise Men 'knelt in sacred terror to confer / [their] fabulous gold and frankincense and myrrh'—and this sense of 'sacred terror' is related to the poet's own sense of the fear which drives men in frenzy to war, the lack of any significant sense of direction in the modern world. War is a violent distortion of the same terror that drives men towards Christian belief. Likewise the reiterated refrains and repetitions of 'A Plane Tree by the Water' suggest in their chant-like rhythms the invocation of a power that will sweep away and renew 'the hell-fire streets of Babel Boston'. It is a poem of exaltation as its title from Ecclesiasticus (24:19) indicates: 'As a plane tree by the water in the streets, I was exalted'. It is the exaltation of longing for a cleansing apocalypse that will sweep away the old world of sin and corruption for the reintroduction of an entirely new world of the spirit. The poem contains a suggestion of some of the self-induced intoxication of a hymn or a litany, so that the sense of triumph seems to be purely verbal. A similar litany-like quality pervades 'The Dead in Europe' which also uses the same repeated line to close each stanza, though in 'The Dead in Europe' there is a significant change of tense in the last line from 'Our sacred earth in our day was our curse' to 'Our sacred earth in our day is our curse'. The poem is a litany spoken by those 'whom the blockbusters marred and buried' without the benefits of Christian burial and who plead for salvation on the Resurrection Day. 'Where the Rainbow Ends', on the other hand, balances its apocalyptic vision ('I saw my city in the Scales, the pans / Of judgment rising and descending') against a final stanza which affirms the paradoxes of faith which console the believer and bring him peace but which also alienate him from this world and its values.

'Falling Asleep Over the Aeneid' is one of the later early poems that marks the end of Lowell's first phase, before the newer tones and styles that were to emerge in *Life Studies*. It is an extraordinary virtuoso piece that gives Lowell an opportunity to display his abilities as a translator and a scholar. Lowell himself was trained in the classics and a large section of 'Falling Asleep Over the Aeneid' consists of an adaptation of lines 30 to 100 from Book XI of the *Aeneid*.[24] 'Falling Asleep Over the Aeneid' is a poem marked by a remarkably harsh archaic power and by a complex coherence of organization. The whole is a kind of verbal mosaic with all the

---

24 Jerome Mazzaro in 'Robert Lowell's Early Politics of Apocalypse', *Modern American Poetry*, p. 348, specifies more closely Lowell's particular debt to the *Aeneid* (XI: 59-61, 67-8, 70-7, 89-92) and states that the poem was in part the result of Lowell's attempt to translate the *Aeneid*.

heavily deliberated details relating to each other and working to hold the situations together. Here as elsewhere Lowell works through a series of juxtapositions: he puts two situations side by side—a situation from Ancient Rome and one at the time of the Civil War—and while he hopes that the meanings will emerge implicitly, he also employs a series of verbal strategies to rivet the situations together.

Lowell provides an introductory note to explain the basic situation of the poem: 'An old man in Concord forgets to go to morning service. He falls asleep while reading Virgil, and dreams that he is Aeneas at the funeral of Pallas, an Italian prince.' The poem is not least remarkable both for its time shifts and its emotional transitions—moving towards the inner world of the man reading his book and moving from the present to the past, from intermingled sound perceptions to emotional and imaginative indentifications.

The first seventy lines of the poem (after the introductory three) are concerned with the funeral of Pallas, with the placing of the pall on his dead body, the body on the funeral car and then the homage and final farewell to the dead man expressed by Aeneas. This richly patterned evocation of the funeral merges with the memory of the death of the old man's Uncle Charles who fought to help free the negro slaves. The dreamer remembers his aunt and an incident of eighty years ago. We are back in fact at the time of the American Civil War when the boy has been holding his uncle's sword and looking at the bust of Augustus on the shelf. This is the connecting point of the dream with the reality. The Civil War has been going on around him; he too has been part of history, part of a great historical event. Lowell does not underline the parallels except in the way I shall mention in a moment—but the suggestion is that just as there was hope for the founding of a New Rome, so there was at the time of the Civil War hope for the founding of a new United States without slavery. Lowell has always seen some relationship between Ancient Rome and modern America; in 'Falling Asleep Over the Aeneid' the two incidents—Roman and American—are related in the mind of the old man. Both incidents are taken to illustrate a profound sense of devotion and responsibility to a cause greater than oneself. The Roman section is sumptuous with an accentuated barbaric harshness interlaced with moments of great tenderness of feeling; the American ending is factual and realistic. The aunt tells her English maid to clip the corpse's nostril hairs and fold the colours on the body. After all these years the old man realizes the relationship between the two occasions: two dead bodies; two moments of heroism.

> It is I, I hold
> His sword to keep from falling, for the dust
> On the stuffed birds is breathless, for the bust
> Of young Augustus weighs on Vergil's shelf:
> It scowls into my glasses at itself.

'Falling Asleep Over the Aeneid' is one Lowell's most brilliantly contrived pieces and it gets its imaginative unity from a remarkable use of bird images and bird sounds. (A similar pattern of images is employed in 'Thanksgiving's Over'.) The poem begins with the harsh sounds of the birds' mating cries *('yuck-a, yuck-a, yuck-a yuck-a* rage / The yellowhammers mating') and the central persona's awareness of birds as sounds is then developed both visually and aurally: the birds' cries are incorporated into the fabric of the verse through a controlled use of clotted consonants, while images of birds move throughout the whole piece. Pallas is carried to the bird priest who has read the future from the entrails of the birds; the sword that he holds has a bird handle 'Its beak / Clangs and ejaculates the Punic word / I hear the bird priest chirping like a bird'. The harlots hang Pallas' bed with feathers of his long-haired birds. . . . Then as the dream state moves into modern America, Uncle Charles, it is recalled, appears 'blue-capped and bird-like'; the boy is standing in a room with the statue of Virgil and a case of stuffed birds on the shelf.

Lowell's poems often work through a pattern of related but shifting images. In this case it seems Lowell is deliberately trying to set up a contrast between the present and the past, between the great world of history and art, and the mundane world of local experience with the impingement of the realistic and the daily. Here we have an example of a poem which attempts to be a criticism of society without at any point actually formulating or stating its criticism. Through a shift of images, a balancing of scenes, a change of tone and of focus, the poet lets the moral emerge imaginatively and implicitly. The purpose of a poem like this, it seems to me, is to create a pattern that sets one reflecting.

'Mother Marie Thérèse' is generally recognized as one of Lowell's most perfect poems. Like 'Falling Asleep Over the Aeneid' it is remarkable for the harsh brilliance of its detail and execution; it too is built up with the intricate care and finesse of a mosaic. The poem is packed with lavishly substantial detail that builds up and creates a complex world of its own. Lowell learnt from Browning in particular how to project dramatic fictional worlds that are self-subsistent, standing clear of the poet's own subjectivity. The speaker of the poem is a Canadian nun, not Mother Thérèse herself; and this indirect presentation of her through the recollections of one of her devoted admirers enables the reader to form a clear objective impression of her—a sense of her presence and behaviour—through showing her impact and influence on others, and the kind of conflicting loyalties she was capable of inspiring. Mother Thérèse is presented as both an aristocrat and a rebel. She comes from an important European royal line and is used to considerable wealth and attendance. She is as much interested in the powers of this world as in those of the next. The vigorous opening lines with their emphatic brisk rhythms convey a sense of the strength of her personality as well as a sense of the monotony of the institutional life:

> Old sisters at our Maris Stella House
> Remember how the Mother's strangled grouse
> And snow-shoe rabbits matched the royal glint
> Of Pio Nono's vestments in the print
> That used to face us, while our aching ring
> Of stationary rockers saw her bring
> Our cake. Often, when sunset hurt the rocks
> Off Carthage, and surprised us knitting socks
> For victims of the Franco-Prussian War,
> Our scandal'd set her frowning at the floor;
> And vespers struck like lightning through the gloom
> And oaken ennui of her sitting room.

Clearly it is not possible to point to every minute detail in every poem, but it is worth observing the effectiveness of apparently simple phrases like 'our aching ring / Of stationary rockers' in the section just quoted. Lowell uses the static quality of the repetition of 'a' sounds in such a way that the meaning of 'aching' becomes associated with 'stationary'. Sound and meaning combined with the image of something built for movement being held still suggest their tense waiting, and their disciplined devotion, but move beyond this to become a symbol of the nuns' whole way of life.

Like 'Falling Asleep Over the Aeneid', 'Mother Marie Thérèse' is concerned with contrasts between the past and the present—in this case with the passing of a whole way of life associated with the Church and European aristocracy. The poem pinpoints the contradictions in 'Mother Thérèse's behaviour,

> how she'd chide her novices, and pluck
> Them by the ears for gabbling in Canuck,
> While she was reading Rabelais from her chaise,
> Or parroting the *Action Française*.

47

> Her letter from the soi-disant French King,
> And the less treasured golden wedding ring
> Of her shy Bridegroom, yellow; and the regal
> Damascus shot-guns, pegged upon her eagle
> Emblems from Hohenzollern standards, rust.
> Our world is passing: even she, whose trust
> Was in its princes, fed the gluttonous gulls,
> That whiten our Atlantic, when like skulls
> They drift for sewage with the emerald tide.
> Perpetual novenas cannot tide
> Us past that drowning.

Everything about her—her attitudes, her emblems and standards, her letter from the Pretender to the French Throne, belong to the changing world of Europe. In the new world of Canada she is surrounded by the signs of her aristocratic past: 'Our world is passing'.

In the middle section of the poem (reminiscent of the end of the Quakers in 'The Quaker Graveyard') the sense of death is mingled with the sounds of the sea and this undertone that goes through the poem again reminds one of Lowell's central preoccupation with death in all its forms and manifestations. This lament is momentarily interrupted while the nun recalls the pompous figure of Father Turbot and then the drowning of Mother Marie Thérèse herself; then the lament for the dead nun is resumed once more:

> O Mother, here our snuffling crones
> And cretins feared you, but I owe you flowers:
> The dead, the sea's dead, has her sorrows, hours
> On end to lie tossing to the east, cold,
> Without bed-fellows, washed and bored and old,
> Bilged by her thoughts, and worked on by the worms,
> Until her fossil convent come to terms
> With the Atlantic.

These lines expressing a sense of loss, ageing, erotic frustration and sterility, with the emphasis on the destructive and corrosive action of the sea, lead into the last lines with the awareness of the irrecoverable past. The last eight rhyme words— fears, hears, ears and tears—reiterate and drive home the sense of grief and lament for all that is 'past, or passing, or to come'.

Critics are unanimous in their praise of this poem, mainly because it shows such a loving concern for the lives of others and an involved, yet detached response to ways of thinking and feeling different from Lowell's own. There is no doubt that in much of his early poetry Lowell is too closely behind the characters he describes; in many poems he seems more to be projecting his own psychic tensions than dramatically presenting a character or situation. In 'Mother Marie Thérèse' he stands clear both of his subject and his speaker so that her own unique individuality is felt as a presence through all that the nun says about her (only in the section quoted above does the voice seem to be that of the poet rather than the nun speaking).

Randal Jarrell commented with his usual percipience on publication of the poem:

'Mother Marie Thérèse' is the most human and tender, the least specialised of Mr Lowell's poems; it is warped neither by Doctrine, nor by that doctrine which each of us becomes for himself.[25]

Jarrell then goes on to praise the sheer reality of the central figures —Mother Thérèse herself, Father Turbot and the nun who is speaking. But these figures must also be seen as part of the multiplicity of facts which Lowell uses to control and frame the poem's intense concern with the fact of death itself. The achieved objectivity of the whole is also apparent if one compares this poem with 'The Quaker Graveyard'. 'Mother Marie Thérèse' is likewise an elegy for a drowned person; but where 'The Quaker Graveyard' comments on *the* world—the world of war and materialism, and spiritual greed and pride—'Mother Marie Thérèse' is a poem about *a* world—a vanishing world, its value and relationships—and it perhaps succeeds in touching us more directly and immediately for that very reason. 'The Quaker Graveyard' asserts and proclaims with rhetorical bravura; 'Mother Marie Thérèse' is a portrait that draws us into a world. And while it is a poem about the decline of the monarchy and the failing power of the Church in the modern world, it succeeds in communicating a sense of these things through the presentation of a particular character in a particular place. The sense of loss and lament at the fact of death is individualized and intensified and we cannot forget that the nun who speaks is also approaching the close of life.

The poems I have been discussing are all examples of Lowell's early work; poems of the first phase of his development written after his conversion to Catholicism. They have some features in common. They are either poems of character or poems of narration interwoven with meditations on religious, usually apocalyptic themes. All of them are extremely elaborate and contrived in their patterns of imagery and structure; they are profuse, even sometimes overpacked in detail; they are often compact and recondite in

[25] Review of *The Mills of the Kavanaughs* reprinted in Parkinson (ed.), *Robert Lowell*, pp. 99-100.

allusion; and they tend to be intellectually ordered verbal constructions using a multiplicity of facts to control and frame a basic, almost overwhelming concern with the unpredictable power of an incomprehensible God and a sense of grief and anguish at the fact of death itself. Most of these poems are closely indebted to other poems and poets of the past, not in any facilely imitative way but in a manner that provokes comparison with the poems of the past and which finds strength through the imitation. These poems are elevated in tone, often strident and over insistent. Written at a high declamatory pitch, they are often used to voice prophecy, denunciation, apocalyptic warnings. In these early poems Lowell works through force and impact, through situations of conflict and tension. His early poems are largely concerned with aspects of American history—with the relation between the present and the past and its sense of inherited guilts and burdens. They lament the way the promises of the past have not been fulfilled; they see the modern world heading towards disorder and destruction.

Apart from the consistent connoisseur's delights that emerge everywhere in Lowell's early poetry, particularly through the variety of sound patterns that he employs, two final impressions stand out. The best of the early poems are those with a specific central figure associated with an historical phase—like 'Mr Edwards and the Spider', 'Mother Marie Thérèse' and 'Falling Asleep Over the Aeneid' and 'Thanksgiving's Over'—where some aspect of the human situation is focused in a character around and through whom concrete detail accumulates. Otherwise there is a tendency for feeling to inflate itself, surge on and project itself through objects incapable of bearing this weight and charge and therefore of transforming and thus poetically communicating the feeling. This is, in my view, the cause of the final sense of frustration and nagging dissatisfaction one feels with 'The Quaker Graveyard in Nantucket' as a whole. In other poems feeling, needing something in which to clothe itself rather than declare itself, veils itself, literally, in obscure references and literary allusions which fail to give it the unique definition of poetic identity. Poems like 'Between the Porch and the Altar', and *The Mills of the Kavanaughs* provide exceptional moments of crystallization of feeling around characters, but the outlines tend to dissolve.

Life Studies (1959)

The years following 'Mother Marie Thérèse' and *The Mills of the Kavanaughs* were a time of personal crisis and change for Lowell in different areas of his life. He was divorced from Jean Stafford in 1948 and married Elizabeth Hardwick in 1949; his father died in 1950 and his mother in 1954; he himself was subject to mental breakdown, and he renounced his Roman Catholicism. During this period Lowell seems to have written little new poetry: Staples records eight poems printed in 1953 and 1954, including 'Beyond the Alps', 'Inauguration Day: 1953', 'A Mad Negro Confined at Munich' and the pieces dedicated to Ford Madox Ford and George Santayana. There are no further publications listed from Spring 1953 to Winter 1958 when 'Memories of West Street and Lepke' appeared in *Partisan Review*, along with 'Man and Wife' and 'Skunk Hour'.[1] Lowell has commented in a number of different interviews on how he started to react against his own early work, coming to feel that it was 'distant, symbol-ridden and wilfully difficult':

> By the time I came to *Life Studies* I'd been writing my autobiography and also writing poems that broke meter. I'd been doing a lot of reading aloud. I went on a trip to the West Coast and read at least once a day and sometimes twice for fourteen days, and more and more I found that I was simplifying my poems. If I had a Latin quotation I'd translate it into English. If adding a couple of syllables in a line made it clearer I'd add them, and I'd make little changes just impromptu as I read. That seemed to improve the reading. . . . And I began to have a certain disrespect for the tight forms. If you could make it easier by adding syllables, why not? And then when I was writing *Life Studies*, a good number of the poems were started in very strict meter, and I found that, more than the rhymes, the regular beat was what I didn't want.[2]

And in another interview, he said,

> I began to paraphrase my Latin quotations, and to add extra syllables

---

1 See Staples, *Robert Lowell*, pp. 112-13.
2 See Parkinson (ed.), *Robert Lowell*, p. 18.

to a line to make it clearer and more colloquial. I felt my old poems hid what they were really about, and many times offered a stiff, humorless and even impenetrable surface. I am no convert to the "beats." I know well too that the best poems are not necessarily poems that read aloud. Many of the greatest poems can only be read to one's self, for inspiration is no substitute for humor, shock, narrative and a hypnotic voice, the four musts for oral performance. Still, my own poems seemed like prehistoric monsters dragged down into the bog and death by their ponderous armour. I was reciting what I no longer felt. What influenced me more than San Francisco and reading aloud was that for some time I had been writing prose. I felt that the best style for poetry was none of the many poetic styles in English, but something like the prose of Chekhov or Flaubert.[3]

That Lowell's work was becoming top-heavy is clear enough from a poem like *The Mills of the Kavanaughs*. As Jerome Mazzaro noted, 'The steadily increasing number of levels on which Lowell compelled his material to interact made it seem only a matter of time before he would eventually reach a point where exhaustion would triumph and his style fragment'.[4]

Inevitably a new Robert Lowell began to emerge—the Robert Lowell of *Life Studies* (1959), a writer who was no longer concerned with overtly apocalyptic themes, with Boston as hell, but a rather wry, unemphatic poet who took the facts and figures of his own family and turned them into accurate and intricate poems of ironic affection, judgment and tenderness. The change is essentially one of style rather than of preoccupation because the larger concerns—American society, the figures of his family, the problems of the self, the fact of death—remain the same. Compared with the earlier poems, the pieces in *Life Studies* are more immediate in their impact, concerned with sensations, sights, sounds and feelings; they aim at an undiluted direct presentation of experience. They largely eschew Christian doctrine and they abandon recondite mythical references although they still abound in multiple literary allusions. However strong their confessional content and their effect of immediacy of experience, for which they have been variously praised and condemned, each single poem is a highly ordered lapidary verbal structure, a work of intricate contrivance and cunning.

Although they were not originally written in the order in which they were finally assembled, the fifteen poems in *Life Studies* form a closely connected sequence and are to be read as a coherently

3 Ibid., p. 132.
4 Jerome Mazzaro, 'Robert Lowell and the Kavanaugh Collapse', *University of Windsor Review*, 5, 1969-70, p. 2.

organized structure, a *livre composé*. (In discussing 'Life Studies' I am referring to part four of the volume entitled *Life Studies*, a section which is itself divided into two further subsections.) It has been suggested convincingly that the whole is best read as a miniature novel, a *Bildungsroman* or a condensed American *Prelude* in verse,[5] and Lowell has acknowledged in various interviews that the example of some of the great prose-writers such as Tolstoy, Flaubert and Chekhov was influential at the time *Life Studies* was conceived.

The poems form a miniature family chronicle and fall into three main interrelated clusters each centring on one generation of the Lowell family. The first three poems—'My Last Afternoon with Uncle Devereux Winslow', 'Dunbarton' and 'Grandparents'— deal with Lowell's boyhood relationship with his grandparents; the next six poems—'Commander Lowell', 'Terminal Days at Beverly Farms', 'Father's Bedroom', 'For Sale', 'Sailing Home from Rapallo', and 'During Fever'—deal primarily with aspects of his parents' lives and their various tensions and difficulties; the last six poems —'Waking in the Blue', 'Home After Three Months Away', 'Memories of West Street and Lepke', 'Man and Wife', 'To Speak of the Woe that is in Marriage' and 'Skunk Hour'—deal directly with aspects of Lowell's adult experience as a conscientious objector and himself as a father, and his personal psychological and marital problems, his sense of alienation and isolation. There is a further subdivision in this final group, the last four poems from 'Memories of West Street and Lepke' to 'Skunk Hour' standing in a division by themselves. This special grouping does not seem to affect the overall design of the whole but to stem from the fact that they were the first poems written in the group. These four poems show Lowell as an adult, facing his own adult experience apart from the other members of his family. Lowell said in an interview with A. Alvarez,

> The poems came in two spurts. The first was more intense when two-thirds of the autobiographical poems were written. This was a period of, at most, three months. Then there was a second period which finished that group and filled in blank spaces.[6]

There is a progressive movement inwards throughout the sequence, from the well-situated and externally securely established

5 Herbert Leibowitz, 'Robert Lowell: Ancestral Voices', *Salmagundi*, 1, 4, 1966-7, p. 37.
6 Ian Hamilton (ed.), *The Modern Poet*, pp. 188, 189. See also Staples, *Robert Lowell*, p. 113, for chronological listing of the publication dates of the separate poems in *Life Studies*.

members of the older generation to the highly self-conscious, self-critical younger generation, from the world of the fractious only child to the isolated adult consciousness of 'Skunk Hour'. The poems plot a progress from the disciplined ordered world of the grandparents, through the progressive decline of the world of the parents—a world without faith, socially insecure and where time is filled in with substitutes for the lack of vocational fulfilment or necessary responsibilities. The third generation is that of the fictionalized Lowell, the *poète maudit* in search of his own identity, questing for authentic, existential values, under the detritus of failure, among the shells of status and the wreck of faith and hope. There is a fruitful irony in the title, since, as Christopher Ricks first pointed out,[7] although they are called *Life Studies*, each separate poem deals with a death or a sense of psychic solitude and decline. A work like *Life Studies* for all its uniqueness is not without antecedents: Edgar Lee Masters' *Spoon River Anthology* (1915) and its various imitators like Osbert Sitwell's *England Reclaimed* suggest themselves. Recently Charles Tomlinson has asserted the importance of William Carlos Williams's poems about his parents *Adam* and *Eve* for Lowell's development in *Life Studies*.[8] Further research and information will also doubtless bring to light the important influence of Lowell's contemporaries, most notably Randall Jarrell and W. D. Snodgrass, and most readers will be reminded however remotely or indirectly of the Eliot of *The Boston Evening Transcript*, 'Aunt Helen' and 'Cousin Nancy' with their sharp glimpses of Boston society.

The sequence begins with 'My Last Afternoon with Uncle Devereux Winslow', set in 1922 on the stone porch of Lowell's grandfather's summer house. The poem introduces Lowell's love for his grandfather (his childhood feeling was stronger for his grandfather than for his father who was mostly overseas in the navy) and the memory of a summer at his grandfather's farm. He recalls sitting on the stone porch and touching the cold black earth and the warm pile of lime left by the farmer cementing a root-house under the hill. This introduces the binding image of black earth and lime that moves throughout the whole section, the sense of touch and feeling being associated with the child's first intimations of mortality. He also recalls the décor of his grandfather's house—its social and cultural exhibits—the snapshots of his *Liberty Bell* silver mine; the photos of his school at *Stukkert*

7 *New Statesman*, 26 March 1965.
8 See Charles Tomlinson (ed.), *William Carlos Williams*, Harmondsworth 1972, p. 213.

am Neckar. Like most wealthy Americans of his generation and social class, Lowell's grandfather was educated in Germany:

> Like my Grandfather, the décor
> was manly, comfortable,
> overbearing, disproportioned.

The verse here, as elsewhere, at first looks lax and prosaic, but this is a superficial impression: Lowell is an elegant as well as an energetic poet and *Life Studies* is a highly organized work, combining aspects of free verse and imagism.

Part II is a memory of looking at the reflection of his own face and it simply registers a moment of time past, an awareness of growing self-consciousness.

> I was five and a half
> My formal pearl grey shorts
> had been worn for three minutes.
> My perfection was the Olympian
> poise of my models in the imperishable autumn
> display windows
> of Rogers Peet's boys' store below the State House
> in Boston. Distorting drops of water
> pinpricked my face in the basin's mirror.
> I was a stuffed toucan
> with a bibulous, multicoloured beak.

Again one notices how the author registers ironically the child's self-conscious awareness of his social status and superiority. The same irony is present in section III—the vignette of Aunt Sarah ('Family gossip says Aunt Sarah / tilted her archaic Athenian nose / and jilted an Astor') the old maid member of the family with her failed career as a pianist behind her, living 'up in the air', practising on 'her dummy piano' and rising like the phoenix 'from her bed of troublesome snacks and Tauchnitz classics'. This affectionate, detached sketch introduces the theme of failure—the failure of those who seem to have all the advantages and are yet unable to achieve fulfilment:

> Each morning she practised
> on the grand piano at Symphony Hall,
> deathlike in the off-season summer—
> its naked Greek statues draped with purple
> like the saints in Holy Week. . . .
> On the recital day, she failed to appear.[9]

9 Cf. '91 Revere Street': 'Beauty pursued too exclusively meant artistic fatuity of a kind made farcical by her Aunt Sarah Stark Winslow, a beauty too lofty and original ever to marry, a *prima donna*, too high strung ever to give a public recital'.

In these first poems Lowell simply presents the situation—or the images—without any overt comment at all, so that they are left to speak for themselves. The fact that Lowell does not give direct judgments or express his own immediate attitudes has led some critics to comment on the nature of the detachment between him and his subjects and his readers; but Lowell is here aiming primarily at an undiluted directness of presentation, an artistic illusion that will help to convey a sense of the presentness of memory. This is not emotion recollected in tranquillity, but incidents recorded to give an impression of immediacy and objectivity and control. The judgments are all implicit in the point of view. Aunt Sarah is 'up in the air', she 'thunders' on a dummy piano; everything about her suggests a waste of effort, the frantic filling in of time with a movement from total withdrawal to intense but purposeless activity.

Section IV, for instance, begins with Lowell remembering:

> I picked with a clean finger nail at the blue anchor
> on my sailor blouse washed white as a spinnaker.
> What in the world was I wishing?
> . . . A sail-coloured horse browsing in the bulrushes . . .
> A fluff of the west wind puffing
> my blouse, kiting me over our seven chimneys,
> troubling the waters. . . .

He remembers the duck shooters:

> Double-barrelled shotguns
> stuck out like bundles of baby crow-bars.
> A single sculler in a camouflaged kayak
> was quacking to the decoys. . . .

One notices here the effective use of alliteration to fix in sound the imitation of the decoy ducks, and this is not an isolated, though it is an extremely emphatic, example. Sometimes, as in the line about Aunt Sarah, 'risen like the phoenix / from her bed of troublesome snacks and Tauchnitz classics' a complex interplay of repeated and new sounds is used with a Popean or Mallarméan phonetic wit to convey a sense of the aunt's revival from neurotic withdrawal and the almost startling renewal of her energies as she reappears after being in bed with heaps of books and trays of snacks.

Lowell's consistent use of such devices adds to the effect of economy that characterizes *Life Studies* as a whole. Critics and commentators are inclined to be sceptical about 'apt alliteration's artful aid', and certainly in the hands of a practitioner less skilled than Lowell it can lead to coarsely mechanical effects, as indeed it does in some of Lowell's own excessively consonantal early poems. But used with precision and economy, alliteration can strengthen and reinforce meaning and concentrate impact. Lowell particularly uses alliteration to create sound patterns, links and connections. This is what rhyme normally does; but alliteration can do all this without the formality and symmetry of rhyme and with the added illusion of spontaneity and immediacy. Hence the impression of informality, even looseness, that *Life Studies* conveys, but the sense of laconic control and mastery in the art. Alliteration is essentially more dynamic, more galvanized than rhyme; it keeps the charge, the impetus within the line rather than letting it flow to the rhyme at the end of the line. This is not the place for a detailed study of Lowell's syntax, but it is interesting to note as a general impression that in the early poems there are comparatively few end-stopped lines; an almost excessive use of enjambement is characteristic. In the later poetry short lines with very long sentences are characteristic; these are emphatic through brevity and alliteration, but they also convey a constant impression of dropping and sinking, through the lack of end stops which keep the line buoyant.

The first section ends with the death of Lowell's young Uncle Devereux who was dying at twenty-nine of Hodgkin's disease. Again, as in the opening section on his grandfather, Lowell presents the personality of his uncle through the description of his possessions, his appearance and the things around him: the things that a person has help to define the kind of person he is. A passage from '91 Revere Street' is apt here as for the sequence as a whole and indicates the importance of things in Lowell's vision.

> Major Mordecai Myers' portrait has been mislaid past finding, but out of my memories I often come on it in the setting of our Revere Street house, a setting now fixed in the mind, where it survives all the distortions of fantasy, all the blank befogging of forgetfulness. There, the vast number of remembered *things* remains rocklike. Each is in its place, each has its function, its history, its drama. There, all is preserved by that motherly care that one either ignored or resented in his youth. The things and their owners come back urgent with life meaning—because finished, they are endurable and perfect.

Lowell remembers his uncle through the series of student posters with which he surrounded himself—posters of Mr Punch, *La Belle France*, pre-war music hall belles and a poster, almost life size, of 'three young men in khaki kilts / being bushwacked on the veldt'. All of these posters evoke a particular time and place, suggesting the range of the young uncle's interests, a world that like the Canadian nun's is also passing:

> My Uncle was dying at twenty-nine.
> 'You are behaving like children,'
> said my Grandfather,
> when my Uncle and Aunt left their three baby daughters,
> and sailed for Europe on a last honeymoon . . .
> I cowered in terror
> I wasn't a child at all—
> unseen and all-seeing, I was Agrippina
> in the Golden House of Nero. . . .
> Near me was the white measuring-door
> my Grandfather had pencilled with my Uncle's heights.
> In 1911, he had stopped growing at just six feet.
> While I sat on the tiles,
> and dug at the anchor on my sailor blouse,
> Uncle Devereux stood behind me.
> He was as brushed as Bayard, our riding horse.
> His face was putty.
> His blue coat and white trousers
> grew sharper and straighter.
> His coat was a blue jay's tail,
> his trousers were solid cream from the top of the bottle.
> He was animated, hierarchical,
> like a ginger snap man in a clothes-press.
> He was dying of the incurable Hodgkin's disease. . . .
> My hands were warm, then cool, on the piles
> of earth and lime,
> a black pile and a white pile. . . .
> Come winter,
> Uncle Devereux would blend to the one colour.

One notices here the accurate clipped brevity of the sentences that describe the uncle: 'He was as brushed as Bayard', 'his blue coat and white trousers / grew sharper and straighter', 'his coat was a blue jay's tail / His trousers were solid cream from the top of the bottle'. Each image is at once poetic and precise, and each is within the compass of an alert and sensitive child, so that Lowell succeeds in suggesting a child's perception while writing like an adult and immensely skilled poet. The images of horses, jays and cream suggest naturalness, vigour and health, as well as discipline, neatness and control, thus underlining the poignant contrast between the external elegance of his uncle, his sense of personal attention, care and refinement and the sense of being threatened from within by an incurable disease ('His face was putty'). Again there is a contrast between the appearance and the reality of the kind Lowell frequently points to throughout the sequence. The section ends with a return to the image of the piles of mud and lime with which the poem began, again showing how Lowell is able to present the clarity and directness of childhood perceptions with an adult comprehension of the facts behind them. 'Come winter, Uncle Devereux would blend to the one colour' springs from the adult's later knowledge of what happened. 'My hands were warm, then cool, on the piles / of earth and lime' has the banal immediacy of a fact remembered from childhood, but it also has a deliberated force and impact: it includes the idea of warm life and cold death which is part of the poem as a whole and part of the precise memory that Lowell evokes. When Lowell says, 'I wasn't a child at all / . . . I was Agrippina / in the Golden House of Nero', he is referring to an aspect of his childish imaginative life—his sense of knowing all that is going on in the declining family. But the idea touches on the meaning of the poem as a whole: the child's sense of feeling and understanding more than he really knows.

'Dunbarton' pursues more closely Lowell's affection for his grandfather ('He was my Father. I was his son'), focusing on one of their yearly 'get-aways from Boston / to the family graveyard in Dunbarton'. The external setting of Lowell's poems is often a graveyard or a vantage point near an historical monument, a situation that enables him to particularize his reflections on the present and the past and to relate himself actively to the continuity between the living and the dead. In Lowell's poetry, Dunbarton, as Staples points out, 'stands for family history, for tradition, and, of course, the permanence of the grave'.[10] But if the setting is Dunbarton this shouldn't disguise the fact that this is one of the happiest poems in the series, opening as energetically as 'My Last Afternoon with Uncle Devereux Winslow' and concentrating with a certain boyish briskness on his delight in his grandfather's company and his grandfather's equally relaxed irresponsibility in the presence of his grandchild. The poem pinpoints four small specific moments that evoke the closeness and the quality of unforced acceptance of their relationship: the drive to Dunbarton with the grandfather looking like an admiral; the raking up of leaves from the graves and lighting a bonfire to defy the weather; Lowell's stabbing with his grandfather's cane for the newts, with which he identifies himself; and finally his memory of cuddling 'like a paramour' in his grandfather's bed. The poem contrasts the young child's sense of rebellion and isolation with the warmth of his sentiments for his grandfather who found 'his grandchild's fog-

10 Staples, *Robert Lowell*, p. 73.

bound solitudes / sweeter than human society'. The weight of meaning which falls here on 'human' suggests the almost animal-like intensity of Lowell's rebellion and self-sufficiency as a child.

As in the previous poem there is a discreet use of colour symbolism, in this case the colours of autumn—red and yellow and orange; the feeling of a breeze playing over the surface of a pond is enacted and suggested in the line 'over the disused millpond's fragrantly woodstained water' while the clotted vowels in 'I lanced it in the fauve ooze for newts' suggests the slimy thickness of the waters where the newts live and breed, reminding one of the Keatsian 'the small-mouth bass breaks water, gorged with spawn' in 'After the Surprising Conversions'. One is constantly struck by the range and variety of perceptions Lowell is able to concentrate with economy of effect, and also the fastidious choice of words, saved from any suggestion of the mannered or the recherché by their unexpected precision. Fauve is doubtless chosen for its sound, but the French word for fawn coloured also suggests wild animal and relates to the colour of the stirred up water, the energy of the boy's activity and to the teeming life in the pond.

'Grandparents' is not only an elegy for his grandfather and grandmother, but a lament for the passing of the whole way of life associated with them. 'They're altogether otherworldly now', the poem begins, suggesting that they now belong completely to the other world, those adults who were always a little old fashioned to the child while they were alive and who seemed to belong to another kind of world from the one he was experiencing:

> They're altogether otherworldly now,
> those adults champing for their ritual Friday spin
> to pharmacist and five-and-ten in Brockton.
> Back in my throw-away and shaggy span
> of adolescence, Grandpa still waves his stick
> like a policeman;
> Grandmother, like a Mohammedan, still wears her thick
> lavender morning and touring veil,
> the Pierce Arrow clears its throat in a horse-stall.
> Then the dry road dust rises to whiten
> the fatigued elm leaves—
> the nineteenth century, tired of children, is gone.
> They're all gone into a world of light; the farm's my own.

The last line of this stanza contains a reference to Henry Vaughan's poem on death:

> They are all gone into the world of light!
>   And I alone sit lingering here;
> Their very memory is fair and bright,
>   And my sad thoughts doth clear. . . .

> I see them walking in an air of glory,
> Whose light doth trample on my days:
> My days, which are at best but dull and hoary,
> Mere glimmerings and decays. . . .

The laconic literary reference, broken off with the sharp factual statement 'the farm's my own', contains a refusal at this point to linger emotionally on any sense of loss: the dead have 'gone into a world of light', a world where everything is simplified and clarified and freed from the tensions and confusions of the living. The nineteenth century—the world of large families that the grandparents belonged to—has gone. But continuity is suggested through 'the farm's my own'.

The second stanza pictures a disconsolate Lowell in the billiard room, built in the old fashioned way to keep nature at bay. Again the note of poised self-observation and self-criticism without self-contempt emerges: 'I . . . spoil another season'; 'disloyal still'. The awareness, the feeling of insufficiency in his life at a particular moment is recorded, not exploited; and the sense of grief merging into self-pity (sorry for oneself left behind) is finely registered. His grief breaks through as he recalls his grandfather and realizes that nothing will ever be the same again: he is ageing; his grandparents and the world they belonged to have passed irrecoverably away ('Never again'). The reference to the lines of the marriage ceremony in 'Grandpa! Have me, hold me, cherish me' suggest the stability and security he found in his relationship with his grandfather and which was missing in his parents' relationship, while the last image of his doodling 'handlebar mustaches on the last Russian Czar' suggests the larger issues of how much the world to which his grandparents belonged has changed and how it was in fact in the process of changing during their lifetime. The image suggests irrevocable change; the gesture 'doodling' suggests blankness in front of the future. The whole sequence builds up an impression of the changes in ways of life that have occurred through three generations of Americans and the subtle impingement of the world events on their lives; but these changes are always particularized and always related to specific moments of Lowell's own experience.

The poems on the grandparents depict various aspects of a family in decline and touch on the changes that have taken place in American society where the old external stabilities, the securities of social status and prestige have gradually broken down. The poems on Lowell's parents emphasize the failure of direction and the instability at the centre of their marital relationship. Lowell deals with this difficult 'emotional' material with admirable reticence and tactful control. It was believed in Lowell's family that his father was destined to be an important, even perhaps a great man. But his decision to leave the Navy and work for Lever Brothers—a decision largely taken to please his wife—resulted in the financial disaster and follies of his last years. Lowell's father was fired from Lever Brothers during the Depression and all sense of significant purpose seems to have drifted out of his life.

The poem 'Commander Lowell' begins with a reference to Lowell's somewhat exclusive relationships as a child, remembering with nervous energy his mother's voice 'still electric / with a hysterical, unmarried panic', as she read to him from the Napoleon book. His love of lists of names and his knowledge of the names of over two hundred French generals is recalled in sharply rhyming lines, perhaps suggesting their mechanical usefulness in helping him get to sleep; and then the poem moves briskly on to describe his father's actual situation. There is a curious pathos in the awkward alienation of Lowell's father, unable to readjust or adequately to fit in to his new social situation. He is unimpressive as a golf player to the wealthy inhabitants of Mattapoisett summer colony, who assume that because he was in the navy his sport must be sailing; but he is not more accepted or at home at the yacht club: 'Poor Father, his training was engineering', 'he was never one of the crowd'. His decision to leave the Navy brings an upsurge of confidence and conviction, ' "Anchors aweigh", Daddy boomed in his bathtub / "Anchors aweigh", / when Lever Brothers offered to pay / him double what the Navy paid', but he was soon fired; as a psychological compensation he buys himself a smarter car each time he leaves a job. The relationship between the parents begins to deteriorate:

> While Mother dragged to bed alone,
> read Menninger,
> and grew more and more suspicious,
> he grew defiant.
> Night after night,
> *à la clarté déserte de sa lampe,*
> he slid his ivory Annapolis slide rule
> across a pad of graphs—
> piker speculations' In three years
> he squandered sixty thousand dollars.

These lines contain another ironical literary allusion of the kind frequent throughout *Life Studies*: 'À la clarté déserte de sa lampe' is a line taken from Mallarmé's poem 'Brise Marine' with its anchors aweigh nostalgia of the timid domestic poet longing for

the life of adventure and excitement, aware of the dangers of sea-
faring, but responding to the call, the nostalgia for another, more
adventurous kind of existence. As with the other quotations
scattered throughout *Life Studies* these allusions have the effect
of registering an emotional response within a situation, but
allusively, without identifying with it or indulging in it. Lowell's
father was driven to indulge in extravagant speculations as a way
of compensating for the frustration and inhibition of his deepest
longings. The last lines of this poem introduce the motif of
Lowell's father's smile ('smiling on all') and his way of trying to
make the best of everything and contrasts the gestures of self-
assertion of his middle age (his pride in his sumptuously
redecorated house 'converted to oil') with the fact that he was once
at nineteen 'the youngest ensign in his class', 'the old man' of a
gunboat on the Yangtze. This abrupt juxtaposition of two high-
lights of his father's career brings out the nature and the irony of
his decline, reminding one of Oscar Wilde's quip about the
brilliant young man with a great future behind him. Lowell gives
the impression of simply recounting factual aspects of his father's
career, but the juxtaposition and placing of the incidents conveys
indirectly his sense of laconic pity, for the waste and the pathos of
some of his father's failings. The isolation of 'And once' in a line
by itself brings out the contrast between then and now; the poem
finishes on the positive image of his father at his most enterprising
and promising, but the image is doubly qualified by what has gone
before.

'Terminal Days at Beverly Farms' deals with Lowell's father's
decline and death. It again picks up the motif of the smile. 'He
smiled his oval Lowell smile' where the repetition of the vowels
almost enacts phonetically the predictable readiness of the smile
that can be turned on at any moment. The implication is that the
perpetual effort to make the best of things can sometimes cover a
refusal to see things as they are. So Lowell's father goes off each
morning 'inattentive and beaming'. The last five lines of 'Terminal
Days at Beverly Farms' subtly draw attention after the reassuring
smiles to the real feelings themselves, thus investing the banal
words 'I feel awful' with a unique charge:

> Father's death was abrupt and unprotesting.
> His vision was still twenty-twenty.
> After a morning of anxious, repetitive smiling,
> his last words to Mother were:
> 'I feel awful.'

This is a good example of Lowell's use of compressed understatement, the economic ending suggests all that is unassuming about the father and something of the apparent off-handedness of death itself.

The emphasis on the father's smile contributes to the general impression of the father as a touching, childlike, ineffectual and un-pathetic man. He has no sense of his own importance and perhaps his smile is a way of reassuring others. Everything about the father is touched with failure: his navy and business career; his role as husband and father (even his son prefers to think of his grandfather as his father). Elsewhere Lowell picks out small details of his father's life style—as with Uncle Devereux, though at a more advanced age, there is emphasis on his father's life style—his cult of efficiency ('His head was efficient and hairless' again brings out the discrepancy between the appearance and the reality); his pride in his small, social-conscious underhand economies. But the sequence employs a number of subtle cross-references to make further points by implication. For instance, Uncle Devereux's blue coat and white trousers 'grew sharper and straighter', while father wears 'a blue serge jacket and *numbly* cut / white ducks. . . . ' Like the other members of the family the father is proud of his possessions—his ivory slide rule, his 'Chevie', but these are external to any vital concerns or achievements; they are implements of reassurance or a means of keeping up with the latest fashion, like his redecorated house with its 'ceiling roughened with oatmeal'; its 'six pointed star lantern— / last July's birthday present' with its emphasis on the merely modish or newness for newness's sake. This is in vivid and telling contrast with the grandfather's and uncle's idiosyncratic, personally expressive and dated possessions— the Edwardian cuckoo-clock; 'Grandfather's cane / carved with the names and altitudes / of Norwegian mountains *he had scaled*', and 'All about me / were *the works of my Grandfather's hands*' (my italics).

In 'Father's Bedroom' everything is delicate and refined, not masculine like Grandfather's world—'manly, comfortable, / over-bearing, disproportioned'—but white, pastel, oriental, with the emphasis on thin blue threads, blue dots, blue kimonos, Chinese sandals with blue plush straps, the neat, matched bed-lamp and the white doily shade. It is significant that the only real object of lived life goes back to his early youth as a midshipman on the gunboat on the Yangtze, the worn book from his mother now used only to raise the bed lamp. There is the poignancy of death in this piece; the impression that this is all there is.

Both 'Father's Bedroom' and 'For Sale' illustrate the way Lowell uses objects, aspects of décor to suggest qualities of life and feeling. The concentration on properties is characteristic of each poem in the series, but these two are unique in their single point of focus. In a way which is both filmic and painterly, but made essentially poetic through the reinforcement of sound and rhythm, Lowell focuses on the blueness of the room in which his father died, where all the objects associated with his father's trip to China are preserved, as a memorial and as a way of suggesting the man he might have been. It is essentially a memorial to the young man Lowell's father was, charged with a poignant sense of the absence of any reference to what he later became. 'For Sale' concentrates on the feelings of his mother just after her husband's death:

> Ready, afraid
> of living alone till eighty,
> Mother mooned in a window,
> as if she had stayed on a train
> one stop past her destination.

This final image suggests her vulnerability, her bewildered helplessness in an image at once modern and exact, with its suggestion of life as a railway journey. Lowell's artistic reserve and control is remarkable again in this small piece. It has something of the charged economy of a Japanese poem, and it is worth observing how controlled Lowell's handling of this potentially sentimental or painful situation is. Although unrhymed, the poem conveys a sense of austere control and restrained pity—the feeling has been transformed into language.

'Sailing Home from Rapallo' (February 1954) is a threnody on his mother's death in Italy in February 1954. It opens with three lines addressed directly to his mother and recording his own sense of inarticulate loss and grief:

> Your nurse could only speak Italian,
> but after twenty minutes I could imagine your final week,
> and tears ran down my cheeks. . . .

And then the poem shifts abruptly in scene and tone, moving from the personal to an account of bringing the mother's body back to America. The Gulf of Genoa was breaking into flower; the water was like sparkling champagne in the wake of the liner. 'Mother travelled first class in the hold, / her *Risorgimento* black and gold casket / was like Napoleon's at the *Invalides*. . . . ' The emphasis here is primarily on the colour of the mother's coffin, but the reference to Napoleon's tomb at the Invalides reminds us as well of Lowell's mother's (and Lowell's own) cult of Napoleon (mentioned in 'Commander Lowell') as well as serving to suggest the slightly ostentatious splendour of the casket itself.

The poem again works through juxtapositions and contrasts, contrasts between the richly flowering world and the expensively coffined body in the hold, contrasts between seasons and places (Spring already beginning in Italy while 'Dunbarton / lay under the White Mountains / in the sub-zero weather'), contrasts between the social importance of the living and the insignificance of the dead. In describing the grave at Dunbarton, Lowell points to the contrasts between his father's family of self-made men ('Even the Latin of his Lowell motto / *Occasionem cognosce*, / seemed too businesslike and pushing here') and that of his mother's historically more famous family of Winslows and Starks. The end of the poem turns on another irony where Lowell points out that the grandiloquent lettering on his mother's coffin is marred by the fact that *Lowell* had been misspelled *LOVEL*.

M. L. Rosenthal in his study *The New Poets* has commented that this poem is above all 'a poem of humiliation, and to this fact even the elegiac motive is subordinated'.[11]

Broadly speaking this is true enough. But it seems to me that Lowell is more concerned to suggest one of life's most significant ironies: that the dead become things among things; fame of a kind and status and social importance in one place may be totally ignored or disregarded in another. Lowell wants to show the contrasts between the inner world of feelings and the outer world of objects (again the general theme of appearance and reality) and to show the apparently random nature of things as they are.

Lowell is constantly pointing to the trivial, the limited, the frail and absurd aspects of things, and the paradoxical effect of this is to affirm the strength and the will to face reality as it is. Some critics have complained that the tone of 'Sailing Home from Rapallo' is callous; but the flat directness of some of its comments is an expression of the basic attitude in *Life Studies*—that there are no absolutes. Lowell has a profound awareness of the role of relative negatives in life. The recurring discrepancies in style between a way of life and the irreducible facts of life seem to be brought out in the relentless control of the last lines. 'The corpse', (the brutal isolation of the word in a line by itself, so much more impersonal than 'the body' or 'mother's body' or 'mother', so much closer to being a thing) returns us to what is after all the main concern of the poem —the separate dead thing which must be disposed of, 'wrapped

11 See M. L. Rosenthal, *The New Poets*, New York 1967, pp. 50, 51.

like *panetone* in Italian tinfoil'. The poem ends on this dry but touching and homely note, with its suggestions of the bread of life. The last seven poems in *Life Studies* are all concerned with Lowell himself, and aspects of his life and feelings and adult experience. All continue to touch on memories of the past especially his past imprisonment as a conscientious objector and his memories and experience at McLeans Sanitarium where he received treatment during his mental breakdowns. These poems deal with the aspects of his own family relationships as an adult and they all point to the increasing complexity of the society he lives in and of the questions he has to face.

'During Fever' begins with an image of Lowell's daughter 'home from the healthy country to the sick city'—a line which picks up the age old generalization about the values of life in the country and in the town, but which relates this idea quite specifically to his daughter. His situation now as a parent reminds him of his mother and of his relationship to her.

> Mother, Mother!
> as a gemlike undergraduate,
> part criminal and yet a Phi Bete,
> I used to barge home late.
> Always by the bannister
> my milk-tooth mug of milk
> was waiting for me on a plate
> of Triskets.
> Often with unadulterated joy,
> Mother, we bent by the fire
> rehashing Father's character—
> when he thought we were asleep,
> he'd tiptoe down the stairs
> and chain the door.

It is significant that he recalls milk being left in a child's tooth mug and that his mother put out for him what was essentially a child's supper, though he was then an undergraduate.

The third stanza again concentrates on objects, furniture, aspects of décor to suggest a whole way of life and something of the contours of a personality:

> Mother, your master-bedroom
> looked away from the ocean.
> You had a window-seat,
> an electric blanket,
> a silver hot water bottle
> monogrammed like a hip-flask,
> Italian china fruity

with bunches and berries
and proper *putti*.
Gold, yellow and green,
the nuptial bed
was as big as a bathroom.

The image of the room which looks away from the ocean serves to suggest the disparity between the external facts and situation of the family, and its inner sense of unfulfilment, latent hysteria and emotional failure. As throughout *Life Studies* the symbolic overtones are inseparable from the strict realism: the master bedroom looks away from the ocean—from the challenge and change of the sea of life; and we remember that in 'Terminal Days at Beverly Farms' 'they had no sea-view'. It is interesting to note too that the *putti* are proper because they are genuine; but also their nakedness does not offend the proprieties, and the image of the nuptial bed as big as a bathroom again serves to emphasize some kind of sexual failure in the parents' lives, a situation foreshadowed in the detail that mother seems to sleep alone in the master-bedroom. The initial situation of the poem—Lowell with his daughter—reminds him of his mother with her father, and it ends with this brisk and wryly pointed comment:

Terrible that old life of decency
without unseemly intimacy
or quarrels, when the unemancipated woman
still had her Freudian papa and maids!

While remaining specifically a poem about his family and the relationships closest to him, the poem nevertheless comments on changing ways of life and on changing relationships within the cultural patterns of the family.

'Waking in the Blue' is a poem of identification. Lowell begins by describing his morning awakening at McLean's and the various inmates in 'the house for the mentally ill', from the night attendant reading *The Meaning of Meaning* to 'Stanley' (once a Harvard all-American full-back) and 'Bobbie' from the exclusive club Porcellian '29, 'redolent and roly-poly as a sperm whale'. After describing these inmates Lowell projects an ironic image of himself in which he shows himself sharing their characteristics: concern for the body, a slightly dandified narcissism, his own search for the meaning of meaning:

After a hearty New England breakfast,
I weigh two hundred pounds
this morning. Cock of the walk,
I strut in my turtle-necked French sailor's jersey

before the metal shaving mirrors,
and see the shaky future grow familiar
in the pinched, indigenous faces
of these thoroughbred mental cases,
twice my age and half my weight.

But this sense of identification moves beyond subdued irony to end on a larger note of concerned pity and charity, a recognition that they are all vulnerable and threatened by the same self-destructive tendencies:

We are all old-timers,
each of us holds a locked razor.

This mingling and final resolution of tones is prepared for throughout the poem which is a tissue of restrained ironies framed by a number of almost resounding, full-toned single lines. These lines are placed throughout the poem with a certain declarative emphasis:

Crows maunder on the petrified fairway . . .

This is the house for the 'mentally ill' . . .

This is the way day breaks in Bowditch Hall at McLean's . . .

These victorious figures of bravado ossified young.

Such lines have a resonance, almost a quality of statement and judgment that frames the detailed novelistic, partly humorous, images of the characters Lowell describes. There are the usual ironies moving through: the Boston University sophomore reading *The Meaning of Meaning* in the house for the mentally ill, where all sense of meaning would seem to have dissolved; and the fact that Bowditch Hall at McLeans is a place of social prestige— 'Stanley' and 'Bobbie' belong to a social élite which of course includes Lowell himself. They are thus all 'thoroughbred' mental cases. But the social status which distinguishes them from their Roman Catholic attendant and of which Lowell is very conscious cannot hide the fact that the shaky future of the aged is the one he sees ahead for himself. There is a deft and tactful emphasis on the body throughout; each inmate is associated with a particular animal— Stanley with a seal, Bobbie with a sperm whale. Both are associated with images of royalty; Stanley has a kingly granite profile (reminiscent of those carved on the cliffs at Mount Rushmore) undercut by the Victorian golf-cap; Bobbie is a 'replica of Louis XVI / without the wig'. These combinations and contrasts underline their privileged status, like members of royalty in exile, but also the pathos and absurdity of their situation. Again the discrepancy between the appearance and the reality. All this is nervously controlled within a poem that moves from a sense of absence and inner tension of a violent kind ('my heart grows tense / as though a harpoon were sparring for the kill') to an awareness of the prevalence of self-destruction. The shaving mirrors are metal and the razor is locked, to thwart attempts at suicide. The poem ends in a way that suggests that the self-destructive impulse is frustrated, not eliminated.[12]

'Home After Three Months Away' is one of the most tightly rhymed poems of the sequence. The accurate rhymes give the whole a sense of energetic elation, especially in the middle section where the poet is happy to be home again with his daughter. This is a poem which is very alert to the processes of time, change and growth. 'Three Months' is repeated throughout; there is emphasis on the changing seasons, on the poet's age (he is now forty-one) and on the fact that he is recuperating and 'neither spins nor toils'. Every poem in the series is particularly aware of time, period, age and season—'I was five and a half', 'half my life-lease later', 'forty years earlier', 'in three years', 'at twenty nine', 'as early as 1928', 'each morning', 'years later', 'just a year', 'after twenty minutes', 'all night', and so on throughout—as well as of specific numbers— 'a single sculler', 'two or three young men', 'three baby daughters', 'six feet', 'its five foot horn', 'five green shaded light bulbs', 'his favourite ball, the number three', 'with four shots', 'sixty thousand dollars', 'a two minute walk', 'six pointed star lantern', 'twenty or thirty Winslows and Starks', 'sunk in his sixties', 'a boy in his twenties', 'two hundred pounds', 'eight foot magnolia tree', 'a nine months' daughter', 'nine-knot yawl'. This obsession with numbers occurs in all the poems and while it may be related to a childhood fascination it adds to the sense of the concrete and the factual—the minutely precise detail that Lowell wishes to focus on. 'Home After Three Months Away' is the poem most emphatic in its reiterations, with its sense of time put away when he was put away; and though he is now happy and cured, there is too the sense of increasing

12 Glavco Cambon is right: I think, to see in the opening stanzas references to Mallarmé's 'Les Fenêtres' and 'L'Azur': 'Mallarmé's condition of "absence", his obsession with the haunting "blue" of the sky, his description of hospital confinement, are deeply relevant to Lowell's own experience, and he brings the literary source into a personal poem to stress the shock of recognition', *The Inclusive Flame*, p. 244. Similarly the reference to *Moby Dick* in line 2 illustrates how Lowell is able to balance constantly 'ferocious directness of observed detail and straightforward confession with a network of literary references that reinforce, instead of attenuating, the directness'.

enervation, the sense of being reduced as well as cured. Like the pedigreed Dutch tulips, talents and gifts can run to seed and become indistinguishable from weed. In its brief, economical way, this poem is 'L'Allegro' and 'Il Penseroso' together, a manic depressive poem that combines the twin moods of elation and despondency. *Life Studies* is bound together not only by contrasting rhythms of moods from poem to poem and within each poem (a poem often begins in one mood or tone and ends in another) but also by certain unifying images that move across poems. In the previous poem it is emphasized how all the razors at the mental home are locked so that the inmates cannot do themselves or others any damage. In 'Home After Three Months Away' the poet is safely back on his home ground and can happily shave himself while his daughter watches. The deliberate but unemphatic concentration on these objects serves to intensify the contrast in his situation. Such a comment runs the risk of schematizing what the poem much more finely holds together. 'Home After Three Months Away' is a wanderer's return, a poem of convalescence and recuperation, a poem that seeks reassurance amid reassurances— 'the time I put away / was child's play. After thirteen weeks / my child still dabs her cheeks. . . . ' Things have changed, naturally enough, yet there are continuities, domestic tenderness and concern, love for his daughter. But this is weighed against thoughts about his own creative future, the future of his talent. He thinks of the faith he ought to have: like the lilies of the field in Luke 12:27 he neither spins nor toils. But the tulips on the small patch of garden down below ('coffin's length of soil' is a grimly apt image combining the idea of a restricted area of growth with the inevitability of death) remind him that everything needs love, labour, and care; tulips and lilies, like his own life and talent, will not take care of themselves. The enervation of the year ahead—noncreative, without activity,—makes him realize that he has no place in society; that, cured, he is 'frizzled, stale and small'—all words which suggest lack of freshness and vigour, a sense of reduction. It is a poem which refuses all consolations, but where its own capacity for lucid unillusioned appraisal is consolation of a kind. It is also a poem like Baudelaire's 'L'Ennemi', where the poet's sense of his own life is inseparable from his creativity as an artist; and this is a feature of the last poems in the group which all touch on aspects of the failure of creativity and creative feeling in poems which themselves manifest superb creative qualities.

71

Like the other poems in the series, 'Memories of West Street and Lepke' continues the recall of past incidents, beginning in the present and then moving back into the past to the time when Lowell was a firebreathing Catholic Conscientious Objector. The poem is a beautifully intricate and subtle arrangement, built around a series of highly modulated, delicately handled contrasts between the author's own past and present and between two decades in American society. The poem works through a series of parallels where words set up echoes and reverberations and multiple suggestions. It avoids all emphasis and rhetoric and all discursive and declamatory effects; it is nonetheless one of the most powerfully critical indictments that has been written about American society—perhaps all the more profound for being so quietly suggested. It is a poem which needs some biographical glossing. Richard Fein has written:

> In 'Memories of West Street and Lepke,' Lowell, the son of a naval officer and the descendant of an old American family noted for its dedication to public and military service, examines his experience as a conscientious objector during World War II. He recollects that emotional event from the strangely tranquil vantage point of the following decade.
>
> Twice Lowell had volunteered for service but twice was rejected for nearsightedness. By the time he was finally called up, America was halfway through the war; and Lowell found himself opposed both to saturation bombing, which especially meant the killing of civilians, and to the demand for unconditional surrender. He refused to appear for induction in September, 1943; and he even failed to appear for arraignment. Finally, in October, the *New York Times*, in an article headed "A 'Boston Lowell' is a Draft Dodger," reported that Lowell had pleaded guilty of violating the Selective Service Act.
>
> A month before, in a letter to President Roosevelt, Lowell announced his intention to refuse military service, contending, according to the *Times* report, "that the Allies were fighting as ruthlessly as their opponents." Denied the status of a conscientious objector, Lowell, as we have already noted, received a year and a day for refusing to be inducted, though the usual sentence was three years; and he served five months in the penitentiary in Danbury, Connecticut. In fixing the sentence, the judge told Lowell, "You are one of a distinguished family, and this will mar your family traditions." By 1943, Lowell had become, therefore, doubly a renegade to his family: a convert to Catholicism (in 1940) and a conscientious objector.[13]

This biographical information is *behind* the poem whose main

[13] Fein, *Robert Lowell*, p. 57.

achievement is that it is able to be so finely critical without raising its voice, and so self-critical and so self-aware without self-laceration or self-pity.

In the first stanza Lowell, who 'hogs' a whole house, suggests a parallel between himself and the man 'scavenging filth'. There is a scarcely concealed note of mingled contempt for and ironic surprise at present success; both are members of a highly affluent society where even the human scavenging filth is a 'young Republican'; the idealistic young conscientious objector who recalls his time in prison now inhabits a whole house on Henry James' 'hardly passionate Marlborough St.'

In the next stanza the deft play on words continues. 'These are the "tranquillised" *Fifties*', contains a reference to the growing cult of drugs and tranquillisers in American society; it also refers quite specifically to the social climate of the times, and more personally to the fact that Lowell is himself now somewhat tranquillized after his manic and rebellious youth. 'Ought I to regret my seedtime?' he asks. The question contains an ironic echo of Wordsworth's 'Fair seed-time had my soul, and I grew up / Fostered alike by beauty and by fear' from Book I of *The Prelude*. Again Lowell is implying a similarity between himself as an intense Conscientious Objector in his disordered and idealistic youth and his attitudes now in his forties and those of Wordsworth at the time of the war with France and his later drift into middle-aged conservatism. Lowell posits, too, a relationship between himself and the negro 'with curlicues of marijuana in his hair', linking this up with the idea of being imprisoned in a drug-like state. The whole poem is an elaborate tissue of cross-references.

> I was so out of things, I'd never heard
> of the Jehovah's Witnesses.
> 'Are you a C.O.?' I asked a fellow jailbird.
> 'No,' he answered, 'I'm a J.W.'
> He taught me the 'hospital tuck',
> and pointed out the T-shirted back
> of *Murder Incorporated*'s Czar Lepke,
> there piling towels on a rack,
> or dawdling off to his little segregated cell full
> of things forbidden the common man:
> a portable radio, a dresser, two toy American
> flags tied together with a ribbon of Easter palm.
> Flabby, bald, lobotomized,
> he drifted in a sheepish calm,
> where no agonizing reappraisal

    jarred his concentration on the electric chair—
    hanging like an oasis in his air
    of lost connections . . .

The person who was so out of things is now at the centre of his
society in so far as it can be said to have a centre or a core; the
laundry image of the opening stanza connects with the later
memory of Czar Lepke 'piling towels on a rack / or dawdling off
to his little cell full / of things forbidden the common man' which
in turn refers back to the opening stanza where 'even the man /
scavenging filth in the back alley trash cans / has two children, a
beach wagon, a helpmate'. The poem works through a series of
subtle connections that suggest relationships between the 'forties
and the 'fifties; but to spell it out in this way is to schematize and
simplify and hence perhaps even do damage to a remarkably fine
poem. Lepke's sheep-like drift towards death becomes an image of
the Eisenhower years in American society, itself falling apart,
centreless. What is one to make of a society that imprisons together
the killer and the man who refuses to kill, the young poetic rebel
who is all mind, so to speak, and the killer who is 'flabby, bald,
lobotomized'? Society has no real place for those who do not fit
into its structures and is incapable of respecting the fine discri-
minations that the poem is concerned with. The poem is about
lost connections ('things fall apart, the centre will not hold' is
Yeats's more rhetorical formulation) and is Lowell's own 'agoniz-
ing reappraisal' of the two decades of American history he has
lived through as an adult. We sense immediately the difference
between Lowell's situation and that of the gangster and the toughs
he remembers coming in contact with; he can reassess his situa-
tion; he is capable of an 'agonizing reappraisal'. The note of identi-
fication is close enough for this to emerge without arrogance or
presumption; and the last line, the sense of 'lost connections'
applies just as much to the poet and his relationship to his own
past as to the other inmates. The drift and formlessness that the
poet apprehends at the centre of life includes himself, and one
cannot forget, reaching the final image of Lepke, 'flabby, bald,
lobotomized', the two previous poems which refer to Lowell's own
three months in a mental hospital. The poem is not only about
what is past, but as the opening image of his daughter reminds us
('young enough to be my granddaughter'), of what is ahead.
    The two poems that follow, 'Man and Wife' and 'To Speak of
the Woe that is in Marriage' are the most frankly sexual poems
in the series, dealing directly with complex marital relationships.
The nature of the sexual relationships between the parents and

the uncle and aunt are suggested indirectly in earlier poems; but these two poems are explicit in detail and are part of the attempt of the series to bring us to terms with the persona's adult experience. 'Man and Wife' begins with the motif of drugs carried over from the previous poem ('Tamed by *Miltown*') and the motif of Mother's bed which has been inherited and which inevitably reminds us of the frustrated relationship between the parents presented in the poems in *Life Studies* and in the prose section '91 Revere Street'. Again, as in the previous poems, the movement is between past and present. Like 'Memories of West Street and Lepke', it balances images of past romanticism and idealism against present realism and awareness, comparing his 'boiled and shy and poker-faced' approach to his wife when he first met her twelve years ago to a sleepless, loveless night when she has helped him through an attack of something approaching madness. It is a highly unconventional love poem, a tribute to the man's close dependency on his wife, registering the force of her anger and rebuke as she tries to save him from himself. A poem about an intensely disordered state, it is remarkable for its controlled energetic opening couplets and its strong monosyllabic rhymes throughout so that the intensity of the feeling corresponds to the love and the fullness of the wife's concern. Like some of Donne's poetry this unconventional tribute is full of unexpected passion and intensity.

'To Speak of the Woe that is in Marriage' is more impersonal in structure and mode. Cast in the form of an inner monologue, it started as an imitation of Catullus and takes its title from 'The Wife of Bath's Prologue'—the wife resentfully reflecting on her husband's infidelities. It has an extraordinary dramatic force suggesting something of the wife's 'electric, hysterical' panic. The superb final image 'Gored by the climacteric of his want / he stalls above me like an elephant' suggests the clumsy brutality of the husband's lovemaking, while 'stalls' suggests both his awkward positioning for the act of love and his failure to give his wife sexual satisfaction. 'Elephant' combines a phallic suggestion with the sense of heavy awkwardness. It is a poem of a woman's radical dissatisfaction with her lot, where all respect and concern between the couple have disappeared. The voice of the poem is shrill with contempt and a lethally alert watching.

'Skunk Hour' brings the sequence to a close and unites some of its themes. The poem itself plots a sequence of dissolution and decline, moving from the impersonal social situation and consideration into the personal inner world of the narrator with an emerging sense of resolution and new self-definition. As in the other poems in the sequence Lowell points to the change in life styles that is happening at Nautilus Island. He takes three representative figures of the modern world, all of whom depend on money in one way or another and who represent money values. The hermit heiress with her inherited wealth represents decaying tradition; the summer millionaire represents the get-rich-quick world of modern affluence; the homosexual decorator is a representative of inauthentic life, dependent on the fluctuation of fashion and taste for his livelihood and using the objects of genuine trades (fishnet, cobbler's bench) as part of trendy décor. They are all, Lowell has indicated, typical inhabitants of a declining Maine Sea Town where the poem is set, aspects of its sterility and decay.

The poem then moves into the poet's isolated consciousness— the alienated consciousness of a modern man facing a sense of his own nothingness in the mechanized world of modern society where only the cars seem to make love and the radio bleats out commercialized pop tunes. These are all that the modern world has to offer to the spirit. The poet reaches a sense of rock-bottom:

> One dark night,
> my Tudor Ford climbed the hill's skull,
> I watched for love-cars. Lights turned down,
> they lay together, hull to hull,
> where the graveyard shelves on the town. . . .
> My mind's not right.
>
> A car radio bleats,
> 'Love, O careless Love . . . ' I hear
> my ill-spirit sob in each blood cell,
> as if my hand were at its throat. . .
> I myself am hell,
> nobody's here—

This section of dejection and despair with its sense of complete alienation also contains a literary echo—this time from Milton. 'I myself am hell' comes from Book IV of *Paradise Lost*, and refers to Satan's excruciating awareness of his own alienated self-consciousness, his sense of being excluded from the pure wholesome world of Adam and Eve. There may also be a reference to Sartre's famous statement 'Hell is other people' contained in the placing of the two lines together:

> I myself am hell,
> nobody's here

76

It is at this point that the skunks appear, searching for food in the moonlight:

> They march on their soles up Main Street:
> white stripes, moonstruck eyes' red fire
> under the chalk-dry and spar spire
> of the Trinitarian Church.
>
> I stand on top
> of our back steps and breathe the rich air—
> a mother skunk with her column of kittens swills the
>   garbage pail.
> She jabs her wedge-head in a cup
> of sour cream, drops her ostrich tail,
> and will not scare.

At first the skunks appear as a kind of ominous invasion walking up Main Street like an army; then they become reassuringly part of the normal world. At rock bottom, when all else has gone, there are still the skunks: they represent vitality and continuity among the wreck and rubbish of things.

The poem is about a society in decline, about a world progressively drained of its inner resources. But in the animals—skunks at that—Lowell sees some possibiltiy of survival, some vital continuing of the life force. The poem ends then with an affirmation, a hard, curiously ambiguous one, but a toughly positive one nevertheless. Even among the rubbish of things or of the faced nothingness of the self one can find a sense of persistence, the sheer will to live and endure and accept things as they are. It is one of the paradoxes of this piece that while it presents aspects of an exhausted, highly self-questioning personality, the poem itself is confident, sure of itself and alert to every possible artistic effect. This may be partly due to the fact that while the poems explore and expose negative aspects of the self, they are without any element of self-distrust. Self-distrust can be projected in a poem through a persona as in Eliot, or mythologized or dramatized as in Tennyson or Browning; it cannot be presented directly as a subject in itself. Thus the bracing sense of courage, clarity and conviction that emerges from these pieces: they trust the reader (and themselves as poems) and because nothing is spared nothing is evaded.

In reading *Life Studies* as a whole it is important to observe the threefold pattern that moves through it. In this sequence Lowell takes aspects of his family experience and gives it representative significance; in fifteen poems he presents us with a concentrated cross-section of American culture from 1910 to 1959, presents us with a family album that sums up a whole phase of American history and the changes of attitude within its society. Lowell succeeds in evoking both the physical background and the mental preconceptions of representative social milieux to show the changes that have occurred through three generations. He employs carefully selected minute details to sketch in times and places and he uses throughout combinations and contrasts with overlaps and reversals. I have already mentioned the importance of literary allusion and cross-references throughout the whole. In the sequence every separate detail counts and plays its role, enabling Lowell to work with concentrated economy. To mention two examples: Lowell succeeds in telling us much about his generations through his reference to cars which reflect changing attitudes towards status symbols and possessions. The grandparents had to have a Pearce Arrow, given their social status there was no choice for them but to have the most prestigious car available. Significantly enough it is kept in a horse-stall: the car is replacing the horse and buggy and introducing all the changes into urban America that Lowell comments on elsewhere ('A thousand Fords are idle here in search of a tradition' and 'parking spaces luxuriate'). Lowell's father's choice of a car is governed by compulsively compensatory self indulgence ('Whenever he left a job, / he bought a smarter car' and 'his best friend was his little black *Chevie*'); while the persona's car is merely functional—a Tudor Ford that serves its purpose of getting him from one place to another.

A similarly unifying reference is that to popular songs placed through the sequence. The first reference is to 'Summertime' from Gershwin's *Porgy and Bess* which suggests some kind of nostalgia for a dying pastoral world; the second is to 'Anchors Aweigh', the official Navy song (originally composed for Lowell's father's class, according to '91 Revere Street'), ironically sung by his father when he left the Navy to work for Lever Brothers and thus embarked on the frustrations and disasters of his later career; the third is to 'Love O Careless Love', a popularized folk song sung on the commercial radio in a world without much purpose or love, but again serving to suggest a longing for love's unity as opposed to the isolation and detached despair of the central figure passing through his dark night of the soul. There are other patterns that unify the sequence, above all that of the seasons: the cycle moves from late summer to late summer. Lowell, who works with surfaces like a novelist, uses detail again like a novelist to set up prolonged suggestive resonances throughout the whole.[14] *Life Studies* is a consciously and deliberately patterned book full of a multiplicity of authenticating facts which themselves question and criticise the culture they reflect.

[14] Since the above chapter was written I have read Marjorie G. Perloff's remarkable article 'Realism and the Confessional Mode of Robert Lowell', *Contemporary Literature*, II, 1970, pp. 470-87 in which she pursues this issue further. Two paragraphs are of particular importance: 'Names of persons and places, settings, objects, and key incidents in one poem are woven into the total fabric which becomes something like a novel, but a novel conceived in spatial rather than in temporal terms. In weaving together "the vast number of remembered *things*", Lowell creates what Yeats called "the tradition of myself"' (p. 482). She adds further: 'By presenting his parents in terms of a metonymic series of objects, Lowell creates a devastating image of a tradition gone sour. Father's "rhino" chair and Mother's monogrammed hot water bottle stand metonymically for the materialistic debasement of the American dream, the dream of the Mayflower Lowells and Winslows. . . . '

For the Union Dead (1964)

For the Union Dead (1964) has many features, thematic and stylistic, in common with the poems in *Life Studies*; the title-poem itself is taken over from the paperback edition of the preceding book, where it first appeared under the title 'Colonel Shaw and the Massachusetts' 54th'. *For the Union Dead* does not convey the same immediate impression of a unified book that *Life Studies* does. This led various critics to comment at the time of its appearance on the somewhat provisional nature of the poems as a whole. There was the suggestion that it merely contained a series of short pieces, random notations, sketches and fragments left over from the *Life Studies* phase and brought together to lend weight and support to the title poem. This view no longer commands wide assent, and *For the Union Dead* has come to be recognized as a book that has its own order and unity, its own contacts with Lowell's past works and its own connecting threads with future developments. Lowell commented in a recent interview:

> Depression's no gift from the Muse . . . But often I've written [in a period of depression], and wrote one whole book—*For the Union Dead* —about witheredness. It wasn't acute depression, and I felt quite able to work for hours, write and rewrite. Most of the best poems, the most personal, are gathered crumbs. I had better moods, but the book is lemony, soured and dry, the drouth I had touched with my own hands. That too may be poetry—on sufferance.[1]

Some critics, of whom Gabriel Pearson is the most important, have even come to see this volume as 'the nub of the matter, the sustained moment in which the whole Lowell enterprise comes into focus'. In what is still the most significant single essay on Lowell's work, Pearson further argues that *For the Union Dead* is 'the logical and conscious culmination of Lowell's effort to regenerate

---

[1] *The Review*, No. 26, Summer 1971, p. 27.

and to demystify his own literary career'.[2] The later poetry, he goes on to argue convincingly,

> can be construed as a deliberate discipline of abstention, an effort to recover for his poetry natural limits and lineaments, by touching without violence, greed or repudiation what is alien in nature. Lowell's mature poetry represents a calculated deflation of afflatus. It abandons itself, in the interest of sane, viable living, to the practice of reduced scales and, not without reluctance, of diminished pretension.[3]

One thus sees *For the Union Dead* as a stage in the poet's growth of self-knowledge and self-mastery which is at the same time an increased mastery of the various resources of his art.

Without wishing to schematize the collection as a whole or to impose any false sense of unity on disparate and fully self-contained lyrics, one can nevertheless see how the poems spring out of the initial preoccupations of *Life Studies* and how they mark a point of progression from that volume. Most of the lyrics—especially 'Water', 'The Old Flame', 'Middle Age', 'The Scream', 'The Lesson', 'Those Before Us', 'Eye and Tooth', 'Alfred Corning Clark', 'Child's Song' and 'Returning'—are in different ways concerned with memory, with coming to terms with aspects of the past or with relating or reconciling something in past experience with a present state, or simply trying to preserve the memory of a past moment. It is no accident that in these poems the word 'remember' occurs frequently—as an intimate questioning as in 'Water' or 'The Old Flame'; as a direct statement, as in 'Returning', 'But I remember its former fertility'; as personal admonition as in 'Tenth Muse', 'Yes, yes, I ought to remember Moses'; or else by implication, suggestion, understatement or basic situation in the other poems. It is an attempt to salvage significant moments from time past. A line from 'Caligula'—'What can be salvaged from your life'—might well be adapted as an epigraph for the whole collection.

The first poem, 'Water', prepares this theme well.[4] In the past, commentators assumed this piece was based on a memory of Lowell and his first wife, but a new version printed in *Notebook* as one

---

2 Robert Lowell, *The Review*, No. 20, March 1969, p. 3; reprinted in M. Dodsworth (ed.), *The Survival of Poetry*, London 1970, p. 56.

3 *The Review*, p. 9; Dodsworth, p. 64.

4 Admirable detailed analyses of this poem have been written by John Wain in 'The New Robert Lowell', *The New Republic*, CLI, No. 16, 17 October 1964, reprinted in Michael London and Robert Boyers (eds.) *Robert Lowell: A Portrait of the Artist in his Time*, New York, pp. 65-72; Pearson; 'Robert Lowell', and the reviewer in *Times Literary Supplement*, 1 July 1965.

of 'Four Poems for Elizabeth Bishop' and entitled 'Water 1948'[5] makes it clear that it refers to Elizabeth Bishop herself. Such biographical minutiae may be irrelevant to an appreciation of the poem itself, but they should warn us against attributing too quickly specific situations to poems about which we can know very little at this stage.

'Water' is an exquisitely complex lyric, a poem of regret and fulfilment. The first three stanzas depict clearly and economically the Maine lobster town with its suggestions of starkness and harshness —'granite quarries', 'bleak white farm houses', 'the raw little match-stick / mazes of a weir'.

> It was a Maine lobster town—
> each morning boatloads of hands
> pushed off for granite
> quarries on the islands,
>
> and left dozens of bleak
> white frame houses stuck
> like oyster shells
> on a hill of rock,
>
> and below us, the sea lapped
> the raw little match-stick
> mazes of a weir,
> where the fish for bait were trapped.

The stanzas themselves are built around an interconnecting series of k, b and p sounds with a wash of sibilants playing across them to suggest the inescapable presence of the sea and its destructive, relentlessly eroding quality. The poem in its restrained, economical way achieves an effect of the actual presence of the sea rather like 'The Quaker Graveyard in Nantucket'. But that earlier poem is richly orchestrated, like a Sibelius symphony say, where 'Water' works with the charged economy of a piano piece by Debussy or Bartok. The poem turns on a 'remember':

> Remember? We sat on a slab of rock.
> From this distance in time,
> it seems the color
> of iris, rotting and turning purpler,
>
> but it was only
> the usual gray rock
> turning the usual green
> when drenched by the sea.

5 *Notebook*, London 1970, p. 234.

The power of memory is suggested in the way the 'usual gray' rock seems to be the colour of iris. The disenchanted repetition of 'usual' is part of what the poem is getting at: the strictly accurate, the uninflated recall of a particular moment, in a particular time and place when two people were together, and something was wrong.

> The sea drenched the rock
> at our feet all day,
> and kept tearing away
> flake after flake.
>
> One night you dreamed
> you were a mermaid clinging to a wharf-pile,
> and trying to pull
> off the barnacles with your hands.
>
> We wished our two souls
> might return like gulls
> to the rock. In the end,
> the water was too cold for us.

The emphasis here is on the destructiveness of the sea—perhaps suggesting that they must part, or that their relationship cannot endure or find some other form. The woman's dream of being a mermaid and trying to get rid of the barnacles leads into their shared wish, their remembered moment of communion. The last line and a half returns to the precise memory of the external scene; the sense of the coldness of the water, the bleak prospect around and ahead. The extraordinary delicacy of this poem needs careful handling—it is itself a triumph of tact, so that to say it is about two people who love each other and who cannot become lovers, or about an occasion of fully shared and comunicated bleakness is almost to damage the delicate fabric of the whole. But what the poem is 'about'—a wish in the past for a future state ('We wished our two souls / might return like gulls') is in a way fulfilled by the poem itself. The poem succeeds in transcending the gap between past and present, and shows the power of memory, accurately rendered, to heal. The simple, plain ending, 'In the end, / the water was too cold for us' brings the poem back to reality with something of the limpid purity of water itself.

'The Old Flame'—'my old flame, my wife'—seems to refer quite clearly to Lowell's first marriage. It is a poem which for all its sense of change and of the irreversible in the past, begins with a flicker of élan and a sense of recovered joy as the poet recalls having driven past a house he once lived in with his former wife.

Now a red ear of Indian maize
was splashed on the door.
Old Glory with thirteen stripes
hung on a pole. The clapboard
was old-red schoolhouse red.

Inside, a new landlord,
a new life, a new broom!
Atlantic seaboard antique shop
pewter and plunder
shone in each room.

The poem concentrates on the externals. The house is still there,
but it has been renovated; there has been both restoration and
preservation, but of course there is no visible trace of all that the
house was in terms of their own relationship and reality ('No
running next door / now to phone the sheriff'; the ghost; their
quivering fierceness with each other; the way 'in one bed and
apart', they heard the plough clearing the road of snow). The
poem preserves this intangible reality with all the tenderness of
accurately evoked memory. It is interesting to note at the end of
the poem the effective symbolic overtone of the remembered
experience of the snow plough. The snow plough is not a fully
fused symbol, but it helps to draw together certain apparently
random, asymmetrical correspondences and to relate to the theme
of separateness and relationship. The two separate lights of the
snow plough, red and blue are apparently disconnected, relating
to the image of two in one bed and apart; the voice of 'flaming
insight' keeping them awake is related to the image of clearing the
road of snow with its suggestion of paths and new futures opening
ahead.

Jerome Mazzaro has commented on the relationship between
this poem and some of the details recorded in Jean Stafford's 'A
Country Love Story' as well as sections of 'The Mills of the
Kavanaughs'.[6] While it is interesting to know about these
similarities what strikes one in this poem in comparison with these
other works, is the sense of recovered health and purpose in the
present: 'Everything's changed for the best'; its ability to record
the tensions of the past without diminution or exaggeration and
at the same time to record present happiness, content and under-
standing.

6 See Mazzaro, *Robert Lowell*, p. 127. Roger Bowen gives further details in
'Confession and Equilibrium: Robert Lowell's Poetic Development', *Criticism*,
XI, 1969, pp. 82-3.

'Middle Age' is also a time poem, with Lowell's father as a constantly remembered, even oppressive presence. It is a poem about the burden of the past and the inability in the mid-winter grind of New York to open into any sense of the future; the way ahead seems blocked by his unredeemed awareness of his father's past and failure. The image of the dinosaur and the crust suggest both the weight of oppression and the fragility of the surface across which he must find his own path.

> You never climbed
> Mount Sion, yet left
> dinosaur
> death-steps on the crust,
> where I must walk.

'Fall 1961' is specifically set, through its dating, against the background of the Cuban missile crisis when there was a widespread fear of nuclear war. As so often with Lowell the approach is indirect, showing the precise impingement of political and historical events on a private sensibility as it lives through a period of personal and public crisis. In a sense, 'Fall 1961' is a time poem; the sense of movement back and forth is evoked throughout, not only through the repetition of the words 'back and forth' but through the rhythmic movement of the whole poem which suggests both the swing of the pendulum in the grandfather clock and the restless reiterated movement of inner worry and concern, an obsessive moving back and forth waiting for the feared and anticipated hour of decision or destruction to strike. The poem is gently alert with a sense of imminent menace and crisis.

It begins with the sense of movement of the pendulum of the clock, and this leads into a sense of the impending doom of nuclear war.

> Back and forth, back and forth
> goes the tock, tock, tock
> of the orange, bland, ambassadorial
> face of the moon
> on the grandfather clock.
>
> All autumn, the chafe and jar
> of nuclear war;
> we have talked our extinction to death.
> I swim like a minnow
> behind my studio window.

The image of glass: 'I swim like a minnow / behind my studio window' leads into the idea that 'the state / is a driver under a glass bell'. Both suggest fragility, a sense of tenuous separation and precarious protection from the vast forces that really control the world. This sense of being separate from the real forces and terrors of the world is developed into a further awareness of his total, bewildered, helplessness.

> A father's no shield
> for his child.
> We are like a lot of wild
> spiders crying together,
> but without tears.

The spider image (reminiscent of the spider image in the Edwards poems) suggests the helplessness of the human condition—'what are we in the hands of the great God?'—but it is a helplessness beyond grief and lament so totally is it a part of this condition. There is the sense of being imprisoned in an unresolved dilemma ('but the clockhands stick'), while his one point of rest amid these reflections is 'the orange and black / oriole's swinging nest'. These lines continue, but humanize and subdue, the swinging movement of the clock hands; the image contains the sense of growth and development. While everything in the world hangs and swings, history could swing one way or another. It is the achievement of a poem like this that it can enact with precise delicacy a sense of obsessive swinging and swaying movement—a sense of total situation—in a final image that reconciles all the different threads of the poem. As at the end of 'Skunk Hour', nature is the one source of consolation and affirmation. It is interesting too, to compare the use of the apocalyptic (stanza three) with that of earlier poems: in this piece the sense of apocalypse is part of the consciousness of the speaker, rather than some end referred to which stands outside his mind, as in the earlier poems.

Lowell is a poet haunted by the sense of the past—as one critic wrote: 'its puzzling disappearance and persistence',[7] His approach to this overriding preoccupation has undergone various changes, but in his later poems one has the sense of the progressive domination of nature images. So in 'The Lesson' a memory of childhood reading and childhood places (the landscape of childhood) is evoked in a state of present awareness of the unchanging repetitiveness of nature. Nature persists unyielding. It is we who change, and though memory tends to fix and make static, as it transfigures, the poem realizes that nature is all continuity. 'The Lesson' says 'and we are where we were. We were!'; while 'Those Before Us' says of those who were part of our past 'They never were'. Both are poems about 'vacations, stagnant growth'. 'Those Before Us' is

7 *Times Literary Supplement*, 1 July 1965.

also a time-memory poem, and like the poem to his father it is about release from the omnipresent sense of the people of the past, probably his ancestors. The poem balances small specific childhood memories of vacation time—adults sewing and playing cards—with his own memory of the wild muskrat that he and a friend tried unsuccessfully to trap.

> Wormwood on the veranda! Plodding needles
> still prod the coarse pink yarn into a dress.
> The muskrat that took a slice of your thumb still huddles,
> a mop of hair and a heart-beat on the porch—
>
> there's the tin wastebasket where it learned to wait
> for us playing dead, the slats it mashed in terror,
> its spoor of cornflakes, and the packing crate
> it furiously slashed to matchwood to escape.
>
> Their chairs were *ex cathedra*, yet if you draw back the blinds,
> (as full of windows as a fishnet now)
> you will hear them conspiring, slapping hands
> across the bent card-table, still leaf-green.
>
> Vacations, stagnant growth. But in the silence,
> some one lets out his belt to breathe, some one
> roams in negligee. Bless the confidence
> of their sitting unguarded there in stocking feet.

The poem records the moment when the past and its adult figures ceases to oppress the memory, drops away ('Sands drop from the hour-glass waist and swallow tail') and is relinquished: 'We have stopped watching them. They have stopped watching'. One notices again how the sound pattern across the stanzas: 'They never were. / Wormwood' contributes to the total meaning. The sound in 'were'—the non-existent past—is taken on into 'wormwood' with all its associations of deadness, rotting away.

There is a striking contrast between the everfresh presence of nature (green) in 'Lesson' and the ghostly insubstantiality of the human past in 'Those Before Us' ('uniformly gray' . . . 'they never were'). 'The Lesson' in many ways strikes one as quite unlike Lowell's other pieces. It almost reads like a translation and is much stronger in its expression of undisguised nostalgia than any other poem in this group. The whole movement of the poem ('No longer' . . . 'Ah the light') is not a detached and sympathetic look back at youth; the poem is not a coming to terms with some specific aspect of the past, conjured up and contained in the contours of a memory (like 'Water' and 'The Old Flame'), but it is plangent with the pang of lost youth and a sort of romantic fallacy, the increased incredibility and poignancy of a process which nature does not share: 'Perhaps the trees stopped growing in summer amnesia'. The poem also uses quite uncharacteristic epithets like 'the high, mysterious squirrels', so different from the characteristic precision, factuality and physicality of most of his descriptions of animals (e.g. of the muskrat in 'Those Before Us': 'a mop of hair and a heart-beat on the porch').

'Eye and Tooth' covers a wider associational trajectory, combining personal images of growth and decay, rot and renewal, points of fixity and points of change. The poem pivots on a submerged pun—the relationship between eye and I, between sight and insight —between physical pain and the tension of consciousness that resists schematization and reduction. A series of associations moves around the sense of the fixity of the past, the weight of the remembered and the inability either to assimilate and absorb or transcend the past itself:

> Nothing! No oil
> for the eye, nothing to pour
> on those waters or flames.
> I am tired. Everyone's tired of my turmoil.

The importance of some of the images for Lowell is attested by a passage in his prose tribute to William Carlos Williams:

> When I think about writing on Dr Williams, I feel a chaos of thoughts and images, images cracking open to admit a thought, thoughts dragging their roots for the soil of an image. When I woke up this morning, something unusual for this summer was going on!—pinpricks of rain were falling in a reliable, comforting simmer. Our town was blanketed in the rain of rot and the rain of renewal. New life was muscling in, everything growing moved on its one-way trip to the ground. I could feel this, yet believe our universal misfortune was bearable and even welcome. An image held my mind during these moments and kept returning—an old fashioned New England cottage freshly painted white. I saw a shaggy, triangular shade on the house, trees, a hedge or their shadows, the blotch of decay. The house might have been the house I was now living in, but it wasn't; it came from the time when I was a child, still unable to read and living in the small town of Barnstaple on Cape Cod. Inside the house was a bird-book with an old stiff and steely engraving of a sharp-shinned hawk. The hawk's legs had a reddish-brown buffalo fuzz on them; behind was the blue sky, bare and abstracted from the world. In the present, pinpricks of rain were falling on everything I could see, and even on the white house in my mind, but the hawk's picture, being indoors I suppose, was more or less spared. Since I saw the picture of the hawk, the pinpricks of rain have gone on, half the people I once knew are dead, and I have learned to read.

An image of a white house with a blotch on it—this is perhaps the start of a Williams poem.[8]

But while the development and accretion of images in this poem, like the freedom Lowell has gained in his later poetry, doubtless owe something to Williams' example, the articulation of relationships and the interconnections throughout are entirely Lowell's own.

The theme of the persistence of the past returns in 'Alfred Corning Clark', though here it is expressed through a fully worked out recollection of someone else. The movement of the poem springs from precise recollections and is a paradoxical celebration—like 'Hawthorne' on 'the true and insignificant'. Alfred Corning Clark was a 'poor rich boy' and the strength of the poem comes from its intermingling of moods: the affection for the school friend and the pain of his death, played off against the humour of the memories, the unerring accuracy of the details that place Clark financially and socially, and the paradoxical opposites that were united in him: 'triumphant diffidence', 'refusal of exertion', effortless success: 'You never worked, / and were third in the form'; and finally referring to their games of chess:

> You usually won—
> motionless
> as a lizard in the sun.

The poem is an attempt to bridge the monstrous irreconcilability of two simple facts: 'You were alive—You are dead'. It is a poem in which the humour is graced with tenderness and the affection has a deeper resonance for the sense of the justice of its fundamental assessment of Clark. It is interesting to compare and contrast this approach with 'Child's Song', where there is an attempt to recapture completely the child's experience, with no relating to or distancing from the present.

Another moment of recollection occurs in 'Law' where the theme is that grace is outside the law. A couplet from another later Lowell Sunday morning poem, 'Waking Early Sunday Morning', is relevant here: 'to feel the unpolluted joy / and criminal leisure of a boy', since that is the sense and experience the poem aims to recapture. 'Law' is a brief celebration of a moment of grace, a moment of vision as the young boy 'bass-plugging out of season' catches a glimpse of a Norman canal. It is like one of the

8 Tomlinson (ed.), *William Carlos Williams*, pp. 366-7. Philip Cooper draws attention to this source in *The Autobiographical Myth of Robert Lowell*, Chapel Hill 1970, pp. 114-15.

moments of vision in *Le Grand Meaulnes* by Alain Fournier to which it might refer, just as 'Going to and fro' refers to aspects to Gérard de Nerval. The poem pivots on a paradox: nature in the first three stanzas is monotonous, always the same.

> Under one law,
> or two,
> to lie unsleeping,
> still sleeping on the battlefield . . .
>
> On Sunday mornings,
> I used to foray
> bass-plugging out of season on
> the posted reservoirs.
>
> Outside the law.
> At every bend I saw
> only the looping shore
> of nature's monotonous backlash.

The moment of vision comes from a human construction in a man-made setting where the artifice of the whole draws all into relationship and gives it significance:

> The same. The same.
> Then once, in a flash,
> fresh ground, though trodden,
> a man-made landscape.
>
> A Norman canal
> shot through razored green lawns;
> black reflecting water arched
> little sky-hung bridges of unhewn stone—
>
> outside the law:
> black, gray, green and blue,
> water, stone, grass and sky,
> and each unique set stone!

'The Public Garden' is a reshaping and rephrasing of 'David and Bathsheba in the Public Gardens' from *Mills of the Kavanaughs*; but where the earlier poem depends on its heavily encrusted series of cross-references, the later poem relies entirely on a sense of atmosphere with the public garden's 'burnished, burnt-out, still burning' to suggest the intensities of a fading, dying love affair. The poem interfuses memory with immediate, sensuous apprehensions and the transition to moonlight at the end is beautifully handled, picking up and relating to one of the themes of the poem—the movement from burning intense passion to present disenchantment:

> Remember summer? Bubbles filled
> the fountain, and we splashed. We drowned
> in Eden while Jehovah's grass-green lyre
> was rustling all about us in the leaves
> that gurgled by us, turning upside down . . .
> The fountain's failing waters flash around
> the garden. Nothing catches fire.

Although Lowell has expressed his admiration for Hölderlin and has claimed that 'Brod und Wein' was one of the sources of 'Skunk Hour',[9] it has not been noticed before that 'The Public Garden' incorporates several lines taken from 'Brod und Wein'.

> And now the moon, earth's friend, that cared so much
> for us, and cared so little, comes again—
> always a stranger

derives from stanza 1 of Hölderlin's 'Brod und Wein':

> Sieh! und das Schattenbild unserer Erde, der Mond,
> Kommet geheim nun auch; die Schwärmerische, die Nacht kommt,
> Voll mit Sternen, und wohl wenig bekümmert um uns.

'Myopia' is another poem about the locked-in consciousness of the poet or persona, and it is interesting for the way it uses Christian symbolism of the Garden of Eden and the Serpent to suggest some central damage, some tarnishing of the self that has occurred.

'Returning' and 'The Drinker' must be the two most ignored poems in the book, yet both deserve particular attention and are among the finest pieces in the collection.

'Returning' is on the revenant theme, and with a beautiful sense of control it balances and relates questions of youth and age, growth and decay, energy and exhaustion, the sense of being out of things with a sense of aching familiarity with what has changed. It is also a poem about memory, of searching for lost clues in one's mind; and if the members of the gang are now bald-headed, in business, the faces and the names he tries to remember 'start up, / dog-eared, bald as baby birds'. The familiar image of the dogs and the bald heads (baldness that links the old man with the baby) unites the poem as a whole, suggesting that inseparable, almost instinctive relationship between the past and the present that the poem is concerned with.

---

9 See Cooper, *The Autobiographical Myth*, p. 65.

Time is also the concern of 'The Drinker'. 'The man is killing time—there's nothing else'—nothing else that is, except himself. The atmosphere of the poem is one of claustrophobia and self-destruction: the excess of drinking and smoking, the sense of vulnerable helplessness; the loss of contact with neighbours and wife leads into the final images of Eve seeking escape from the Garden and the last images of stagnation—the wilting cheese, the souring milk, car keys and razor blades in the ashtray. The poem ends:

> Is he killing time? Out on the street,
> two cops on horseback clop through the April rain
> to check the parking meter violations—
> their oilskins yellow as forsythia.

This is one of Lowell's most perfect endings. The question leads back to the opening of the poem, but after what the poem has shown one wonders indeed if he is killing time—if time is the Baudelairian enemy or simply an image or aspect of some larger despair. The cops checking the parking meter violations assert the dominion of time: we are all living on borrowed time and time must be paid for, not violated; but by a brilliant reversal and extension of the idea the cops also represent the values and morality of public order opposed to the chaos and waste of private disorder: the human city can only be kept in order by the assertion and imposition of external values.

'Jonathan Edwards in Western Massachusetts' combines a number of the themes of Lowell's early and later works, merging his preoccupation—a sense of the apocalyptic with a search for Paradisal moments—with those of Jonathan Edwards with whom he once more identifies himself. The poem's point of departure is a visit to Edwards' home in Western Massachusetts and Lowell's reflection that the world of Edwards' faith and belief has now irrevocably disappeared—'the millstone and rock of hope has crumbled', but the square white houses remain. The poem pivots on what loss of faith means ('faith is trying to do without / faith') both to the individual and to the society of which he is part:

> Edwards' great millstone and rock
> of hope has crumbled, but the square
> white houses of his flock
> stand in the open air,
>
> out in the cold,
> like sheep outside the fold.
> Hope lives in doubt.
> Faith is trying to do without

faith. In western Massachusetts,
I could almost feel the frontier
crack and disappear.
Edwards thought the world would end there.

We know how the world will end,
but where is paradise, each day farther
from the Pilgrim's blues for England
and the Promised Land.

In the next four stanzas Lowell reflects on what Paradise might mean—a great country house or a great garden full of the sense of the presence of God (part of the imagery here is drawn from Bacon's essay 'Of Gardens':

And because the *Breath* of Flowers is farre Sweeter in the Aire, (where it comes and Goes, like the Warbling of Musick) then in the hand, therefore nothing is more fit for that delight, then to know, what be the *Flowers*, and *Plants*, that doe best perfume the Aire.)

But, Lowell reflects, such images of the perfect place are also historically conditioned, and their worlds have now irredeemably changed:

Ah paradise! Edwards,
I would be afraid
to meet you there as a shade.
We move in different circles.

Two images of Edwards' world then follow: that of the vision of spiders and that of the soul of Sarah Pierrepont who became Edwards' wife and by whom he had eleven children. This section points out the contradictions and limitations of Edwards' belief: his tender devotion to his wife is contrasted with his merciless view of humanity as so many helpless spiders condemned to die, and the paradoxes of his doctrines and actions are brought out in the final highly ironic stanzas, where the man who wrote so much denying the freedom of the will is afraid to leave his last flock of Houssatonic Indian children or to become the president of Princeton. Edwards becomes an image to Lowell of that contradictory integrity and fidelity to self and his own values that Lowell has celebrated in other figures as different as Hawthorne, Ford and Santayana:[10] 'furtive, foiled, dissatisfied', with a 'shy, distrustful ego'. The reticent hero is as important to Lowell as

10 See Fein, *Robert Lowell*, p. 99.

93

Napoleon or any other military hero. One notices here that Lowell, far from embracing Edwards' convictions from within the poem, stands outside Edwards' ultimate beliefs to present him as a rather pathetic ageing figure.

The next four poems—'Tenth Muse', 'The Neo-classical Urn', 'Caligula' and 'The Severed Head'—all deal with some negative aspect of experience—morally negative experiences like sloth and cruelty, or with some inner turmoil, or are an attempt to come to terms with the monsters within—with a sense of helpless vulnerability or excruciating self-consciousness. 'Tenth Muse' is a poem about the burdens of 'sloth' which because of its heart-felt intensity has a certain vigour and élan. It is a paradoxical poem pointing to the virtues perhaps inherent in *accedia*: the old declarative certainties have gone, the old admonitions are put aside for the greater wisdom of doubt, the richer courage of negative capability. If 'Tenth Muse' is a poem about the death of the will, then there is a sense that even greater stability and security could be found in that death too:

> But I suppose even God was born
> too late to trust the old religion—
> all those settings out
> that never left the ground,
> beginning in wisdom, dying in doubt.

'The Neo-Classical Urn' touches on a latter-day realization that the poet too is as fragile and as vulnerable as the turtles he caught and treated so cruelly as a child. The situation of imprisoning the turtles in the neo-clasical urn in the garden where they eventually died is reminiscent of the moment recorded in 'Dunbarton' where the young boy Lowell caught newts in a tobacco tin; but in 'The Neo-Classical Urn' the sense of total identification between the victim and the older poet himself is more explicit and perhaps more properly comparable with the sense of identification established in a poem like 'Waking in the Blue'; the 'crippled last survivors' prey on the poet's mind as he realizes both his responsibility and his involvement.

'Caligula' is also a poem of identification—identification with the emperor Caligula with whom Lowell has always felt a special affinity, being known even now as Cal among his friends. In 'Caligula' Lowell recognizes his 'lowest depths of possibility'—the possibility of an element of self-destruction taking over and leading him to some final annihilating lawlessness in which egomania or monomania identifies itself with the absolute. He admits that present knowledge leads him to find Caligula a disappointing figure, but he recognizes in him some authentic pain as he relives his last night, his depraved lawlessness, his egotistical obsessed anarchy. He realizes Caligula is to be pitied as a lonely child and an equally lonely man.

The last four poems before the title-piece also form a personal group: all are concerned immediately with the poet's private experience or with members of his family, and three of the poems are addressed directly to his wife. The first of this bracket, 'Soft Wood', with its inscription for Harriet Winslow, is one of the most moving and intimately touching poems Lowell has written. It needs to be compared with 'Fourth of July in Maine' in *Near The Ocean* and is, like that poem, basically a house poem (in a tradition familiar from Ben Jonson, Marvell, through to Yeats and W. H. Auden) since Harriet Winslow owned the house Lowell and his family inhabit in both poems.

The poem begins with an image of the seals in their barred cage at the zoo. Seal packs move past the house in summer and the poet reflects that even in their cages at the zoo seals are happy: they represent the happiness of instinctive animal life. The suggestion of their being the non-reflecting but vulnerable element in life, happy because they are at home in nature and without conflicts in their will, is brought out by the implied contrast with Matthew Arnold's Scholar Gypsy who also represents escape from doubt and the disunities of the divided, highly self-conscious mind of modern man.

> Sometimes I have supposed seals
> must live as long as the Scholar Gypsy.
> Even in their barred pond at the zoo they are happy,
> and no sunflower turns
> more delicately to the sun
> without a wincing of the will.

The second stanza marks a return to the Maine seaport town after two years away: 'Here too in Maine things bend to the wind forever', and this idea of being part of the movement of nature— facing the sun like the seals or the wind like the things in Maine, of giving in to the movement of nature, is celebrated as part of the health-giving qualities of the place. One must, on return, get used to the brightness and cleanliness of the place, the salt and evergreen quality. This sense of natural abundance, vitality and health continues in the next stanza with the images of the juniper berries spilling crystal-clear gin and the healing quality of the hot water in the bathtub.

The sense of continuity and richness is affirmed again at the beginning of the next stanza—'things last'—but already a questioning note of doubt begins to enter: 'there is no utility or inspiration / in the wind smashing without direction' and even 'The fresh paint / on the captains' houses hides softer wood'. Nature can be oppressive in its intensity and overwhelm the mind; a blank, blinding surface that hides the truth underneath. The images of wind and whiteness lead by association into the next stanza where the poet recalls the square riggers which helped make his ancestors' fortune. The awareness of how made possessions do not endure (unlike the elements) causes the poet to reflect that 'shed skin will never fit another wearer'—that nothing lasts, nothing endures. The human body will only serve one person for one life. The sense of the continuity of the natural world—'the seal pack will bark past my window / summer after summer' is contrasted with his sense of mortality in the human world ('This is the season / when our friends may and will die daily') which in turn leads to his direct statement about Harriet Winslow in the final stanza. Here he affirms his sense of closeness to his aunt (she 'was more to me than my mother') who is away ill in Washington, his awareness of the agonies of human consciousness, 'knowing / each drug that numbs alerts another nerve to pain'. The title itself points to the contrasts and antinomies the poem so firmly balances: the fragility and vulnerability of the human in front of the world of mutability and decay.

'New York 1962: Fragment', 'The Flaw' and 'Night Sweat' are three love poems of great delicacy and candour addressed to his wife Elizabeth Hardwick. The first, a fragment, contrasts their urban flat, twenty stories high, as they gaze into the sky, with the world of nature and remembers a painting of tulips they bought years ago. It is a poem about the specific difficulties of a particular situation. 'The Flaw' on the other hand is set in a country graveyard and is a reflection on the future death of husband and wife. The idea that all is possible and unpredictable is balanced against the awareness of the inevitability of death, an awareness which gives particular poignancy to the lines about the lovers touching:

> Two walking cobwebs, almost bodiless,
> crossed paths here once, kept house, and lay in beds.
> Your fingertips once touched my fingertips
> and set us tingling through a thousand threads.
> Poor pulsing *Fête Champêtre!* The summer slips
> between our fingers into nothingness.

'Night Sweat' is a double sonnet; the first section is about the creative labour and effort involved in writing, 'sweating it out' in all senses of the word with the writer's constant fear of running dry of inspiration; the second, an aubade, a morning awakening and a tribute to his wife whose 'lightness alters everything' and helps him to bear the weight of his life. The image of her as a tortoise and a turtle (an old symbol of the animal who was supposed to bear the world on its back) leads into the final tribute to her for her support and for bearing the weight of his existence as well.

'For the Union Dead' which is the title poem of the book, is one of Lowell's most perfect and most finely complex poems. It is a poem whose suggestive power increases with every reading and whose resonance and structural harmony never cease to amaze. Using the freer style of his later modes, he returns to the preoccupations of his earlier verse—the relationship between the past, the present and the future in American society. With this poem Lowell once again returns to his role as a public poet in an attempt to combine personal public themes without the inflation of rhetoric or the dangers and pretences of the grand manner. The poem's epigraph is taken from the inscription on the monument to Robert Shaw '*Reliquit Omnia Servare Rem Publicam*': 'He leaves everything behind to serve the nation'. Lowell changes this form to read 'They left everything behind to serve the nation', a form that includes the rank and file of Shaw's regiment and all of the Union dead.[11]

Like so many of Lowell's poems, this one covers a large time span both in American history and in the life of the central persona. It begins with an image of the old South Boston Aquarium standing in the snow, its windows boarded and the tank dry. Boston was Lowell's home town and he recalls a moment from his childhood: 'my nose crawled like a snail on the glass: / my hand tingled / to burst the bubbles'. The pull and sway of the next lines evokes his sense of regressive longing for that world— not only for the images and moments of childhood but for the non-human, prehuman world of 'the dark and downward and vegetating kingdom / of the fish and reptile'. He recalls by association another 'underworld' image. Last March Boston Common was being dug up. 'Behind their cage / yellow dinosaur steamshovels were grunting / as they cropped up tons of mush and grass / to gouge their underworld garage'—a good example of the way Lowell combines the visual (the steamshovels look like dinosaurs) and the aural (the guttural *g* sounds suggest laboured energetic effort) to evoke the sense of a total scene. The demolition of the old Aquarium, the redevelopment of roadways and the

---

11 See Lionel Trilling, *The Experience of Literature*, New York 1967, p. 964, for further comment on the significance of the inscription.

growth of parking spaces are part of the growth and change of the modern city. One thinks inevitably of Baudelaire's 'le Cygne', especially Part I with its reference to the poet's 'mémoire fertile' and its observation that 'la forme d'une ville / change plus vite, hélas! que le coeur d'un mortel'. Like the swan in Baudelaire's poem the statue of Shaw also seems to contain some suggestion of reproach to the gods, or to the powers that be.

The next stanzas introduce the central reference to the historical figure of Colonel Shaw commemorated in a public monument which faces the statehouse excavation. Shaw represents youthful idealism, the force of tradition, the nobility and heroism of the past. Colonel Robert Shaw was the twenty-five-year-old leader of the 54th Massachusetts Infantry, which was the first colored regiment in the American Civil War, dedicated to the liberation of the American Negroes.[12] Shaw and nearly half of his men were killed within or before the walls of Fort Wagner. According to William James, whose oration at the unveiling of the monument provides some of the poem's detail, Shaw bore witness to the brotherhood of man.[13] Colonel Shaw's body was buried in a common grave with those of his negroes. 'In death as in life, then, the Fifty-fourth bore witness to the brotherhood of man. The lover of heroic history could wish for no more fitting sepulchre for Shaw's magnanimous young heart.' Lowell notes that:

> Two months after marching through Boston,
> half the regiment was dead;
> at the dedication,
> William James could almost hear the bronze Negroes breathe.

The next stanzas describe Shaw both physically and morally: his puritan rectitude ('he seems to wince at pleasure, / and suffocate for privacy'); and his heroism—the power to choose a certain way of life and to die for it. Notice how functional the images are: 'Its Colonel is as lean as a compass-needle' (which suggests his spare fineness and also the fact that he was a leader, a giver of direction). The sense of service that Shaw represents ('He leaves all to serve the state' as the epigraph says) is in decline:[14] the small New England churches remain; 'frayed flags / quilt the graveyards of

---

12 For a very full account of the historical background of the poem see Trilling. *The Experience of Literature*, pp. 960-4; Mazzaro, *Robert Lowell*, pp. 124-7; and Paul C. Doherty, 'The Poet as Historian: "For The Union Dead" by Robert Lowell', *Concerning Poetry*, 1, 1968, pp. 37-41.

13 See Mazzaro, pp. 125-6.

14 Cf. 'the age / numbs the failed nerve to service' in 'In the Cage' *Notebook*, p. 61.

the Grand Army of the Republic'. Tradition decays and is destroyed:

> Shaw's father wanted no monument
> except the ditch,
> where his son's body was thrown
> and lost with his 'niggers.'

(The inverted commas are significant.)

In the next stanza 'The ditch is nearer'—i.e. the last ditch—the end of the world. (The apocalyptic note is more subdued here than in the early poems.) 'There are no statues for the last war here'. Then comes the extraordinary image of the commercial photograph showing Hiroshima after the atom bomb and advertising a Mosler Safe, the 'Rock of Ages' that survived the blast. Through this image Lowell is able to suggest something of the horror of the modern world and of how that horror is trivialized, reduced and made meaningless by the pressures of commercialism. The poem continues 'Space is nearer'—the world is moving more and more into outer space, but at home—'When I crouch to my television set / the drained faces of Negro schoolchildren rise like balloons'—the negro problem remains, whatever is happening on the moon.

The next stanza—

> Colonel Shaw
> is riding on his bubble,
> he waits
> for the blessed break

—picks up the image of bubbles from the opening stanzas about the Aquarium—pointing, too, to the imminent destruction of things. The Aquarium that belonged to his childhood has gone. Cars replace the fish in the underworld garage.

> The Aquarium is gone, Everywhere,
> giant finned cars nose forward like fish;
> a savage servility
> slides by on grease.

In their own way these last three lines are as fierce a condemnation of society as Lowell has uttered. The snarling sibilants are full of contempt—'A savage servility / slides by on grease'—contempt for a society which is violent, cringing and servile in front of money values—a completely materialistic, affluent society which no longer understands Colonel Shaw or the values of one who leaves all to serve the state. Service gives way to servility; the oxymoron 'a savage servility', points up some of the contradictions of modern life: the violence, the passivity. This is a poem sharply, accurately and subtly critical of society as a whole and its growing corruption. Christopher Ricks has commented on

> the equivocation (itself sliding) in 'slides by on grease', where 'on', used here as it is of cars, suggests ('runs on oil') that grease is the fuel as well as what you slide on, both the internal motive-power and the external slippery slope.[15]

There is also the overtone of greasing the palm as well as the sense of sliding by, so different from the uprightness of Shaw, who cannot bend his back. The importance of these two words—grease and service—and the sense of everything having its price is high-lighted by their use in Lowell's adaptation of Racine's *Phèdre* (Act 4, Sc. vi):

> Phaedra . . .
> . . . Leave me, go, and die
> May your punishment be to terrify
> all those who ruin princes by their lies,
> hints, acquiescence, filth and blasphemies—
> panders who grease the grooves of inclination,
> and lure our willing bodies from salvation.
> Go die, go brighten false flatterers, the worst
> friends the gods can give to things they've cursed.
> Oenone: I have given all and left all for her service,
> almighty gods! I have been paid my price!

'For the Union Dead' has some thematic affinities with an earlier poem like 'At the Indian Killer's Grave', but formally the two poems are very different. After the firm traditional shapes of the early work, Lowell's later poems look frail, sketch-like. Technical changes are usually associated with emotional and imaginative changes and I have mentioned some of the experiences that affected Lowell in the early 'fifties. But mention must be made, too, of the general move in American poetry as a whole from closed to open form. This involved the abandonment of the traditional rhetorical structures of poetry in favour of an open verse form—casual, loose, informal poetry which aims to be as natural as breathing. Lowell has been influenced by some of these new developments and his work reflects the changes from the formalist 'forties to the more relaxed and open form of the 'fifties and 'sixties. The highly mannered control, however, remains.

15 *New Statesman*, 26 March 1965, p. 494.

Near the Ocean (1967)

The poems in *Near the Ocean* are among the fiercest and most apocalyptic that Lowell has written, sometimes in their apparent formalism seeming to be a return to the earlier work, though the muted tones and changes of accent and emphasis make it clear that they belong to the later work. Nobody reading them out of order would be inclined to place them among *Poems 1938-49* although they come as something of a surprise after *Life Studies* and *For the Union Dead*. Lowell has prefaced this collection with a note that reads: 'The theme that connects my translations is Rome, the greatness and horror of her Empire. . . . How one jumps from Rome to the America of my own poems is something of a mystery to me'. This remark seems more disarming than is perhaps intended; there is no need not to take it as an honest statement of fact. Lowell has said elsewhere—and it is a statement confirmed by many other poets—'my ear turns up things reason is unaware of' and 'what I didn't intend often seems now at least as valid as what I did'.[1] But there is another statement by Lowell, even more revealing to my mind, about the connection between Rome and America—and one that is already suggested in several early poems and most notably in 'Falling Asleep Over the Aeneid'. The statement occurs in a review of William Carlos Williams' *Paterson*, Book Two, printed in *Nation*, No. 166, 19 June 1948[2] (and probably written about the time 'Falling Asleep Over the Aeneid' was composed):

> *Paterson* is an attempt to write the American Poem. It depends on the American myth, a myth that is seldom absent from our literature —part of our power, and part of our hubris and deformity. At its grossest the myth is propaganda, puffing and grimacing: Size, Strength, Vitality, the Common Man, the New World, Vital Speech, the Machine; the hideous neo-Roman personae; Democracy, Freedom, Liberty, the Corn, the Land. How hollow, windy and inert this would have seemed to an imaginative man of another culture! But the myth is a serious matter. It is assumed by Emerson, Whitman and

1 Quoted from Phillip Cooper, *The Autobiographical Myth*, p. 94.
2 Reprinted in Tomlinson (ed.), *William Carlos Williams*, pp. 165-8.

Hart Crane; by Henry Adams and Henry James. For good or for evil, America *is* something immense, crass and Roman. We must unavoidably place ourselves in our geography, history, civilization, institutions and future.

The key sentence here is 'For good or for evil, America *is* something immense, crass and Roman'. The emphasis here, as often in Lowell's prose, is closer to the spirit and feeling of the later than the earlier work, but it is clearly an idea that has been long active in his mind.

Like Stevens' 'Sunday Morning', which the title of Lowell's poem inevitably recalls, or Valéry's 'Aurore', 'Waking Early Sunday Morning' enacts the inclusive movement of consciousness, and shows what happens in the mind as it becomes aware of its own thoughts and sensations. The basic theme of the poem, the theme that relates and unifies the apparently varied preoccupations of the whole, is that of the frailty of human consciousness, the frailty of the human situation linked with an urgent need to procreate before death, 'to break loose', and move into some natural cycle that will ensure continuity before extinction inevitably overtakes the individual and society as a whole.

The first five stanzas are clear and straightforward enough. The first two stanzas record an impulse to break into the complete physical life of the salmon moving up river to spawn against the current but impelled by the fiercer currents of its own natural life as body and soul wake and momentarily seem to become one. The next two stanzas become aware of the continuity of commercial life. Stanza five is a key stanza. The glass of water becomes a symbol of pure spirit ('silvery colours touched with sky') reflecting heaven, but also of this world and admitting its presence ('background behind it of brown grain') but not corrupted by it ('to darken it, but not to stain').

This prepares us for the next stanza which is a prayer that the spirit can remain of this world but pure, and which quite explicitly works out the symbolic overtones of the previous image. In this connection it is important to note how the glass of water is wet 'with a fine fuzz of icy sweat'. This is purely descriptive of the beads of moisture on the cold surface of the glass, but the vocabulary contains the inseparable sense of the sweat of fear and strain, and this same moisture produces silvery opaqueness, and paradoxically 'silvery colours touched with sky / *serene in their neutrality*'.

At this point of focus on the glass and the wood, the poem moves naturally ('O that the spirit could remain / tinged but untarnished by its strain') into the world of the intellect and adopts the use of rhetoric, apostrophe and abstraction. The poet hears the new electric bells chiming in a nearby church and longs to be doing something else or to be 'anywhere, but somehow else' —lines which echo the refrain 'Anywhere, anywhere / Out of the world!' from Thomas Hood's 'Bridge of Sighs', and the title of one of the most striking of Baudelaire's prose poems of *Le Spleen de Paris* ('Anywhere out of the world!'). Lowell brings out the contrast here between the brash, untraditional new bells and the 'Faith of Our Fathers' which is a sort of anachronistic continuity. But the persona no longer goes to church on Sunday mornings. He recalls the old Puritan hymns he knew:

> they sing of peace, and preach despair;
> yet they gave darkness some control,
> and left a loophole for the soul.

The use here of balance and antithesis is characteristic of the poem as a whole.

These central stanzas are concerned with Lowell's loss of religious faith: exploring the woodshed he sees bits and pieces left over from some early form of worship (a family altar?) and identifies himself as one of those damned by St Paul's precept and example: 'who have not charity and have become as sounding brass or a tinkling cymbal'. This sense of personal loss of faith in the value of external religious observations is associated in the next stanza with his sense of the decline of the awareness of God's presence in life. He is less and less visible; the vanishing emblems of the church seem like things left to console the mad rather than a vital, continuing presence.

The next stanza (ten) moves on to a level that in tone and aspiration recalls Lowell's own earlier work: he yokes together the political and the personal, images from Imperial Rome with those of modern America, allusions to David's victory over Goliath ('hammering military splendour', 'mass liquidations') to convey the sense of some imminent disaster caused by the increase in military growth and power.

The poem again moves inwards away from concern with America's military situation: 'Sing softer', the poet addresses himself. But he is aware that a mere diminuendo will not necessarily bring 'true tenderness'; the kind of renewal longed for seems restlessly out of reach and again a series of antithetical ideas and expressions suggests ceaseless longing for something else, somewhere else. Again he brings his own wish for change and the simple sense of sheer existence—the personal and the public—into line through comparing his own desire to be somewhere else with an image of the President, throwing off the cares of state so that he can relax in his Sunday swimming pool: 'nude, unbuttoned, sick / of his ghost-written rhetoric'. ' . . . O to break loose . . . ' The opening theme returns. But the poet realizes how illusory this intense longing is: all life's grandeur seems to be in escape, in elated moments of release, as with 'a girl in summer', or the elated President suddenly free from the cares of state. But this is deceptive. 'No weekends for the gods now', 'wars flicker', 'fresh breakage', 'chance assassinations', 'man thinning out his kind'. 'There is no release, no escape such as you long for'—the words from 'Mr Edwards and the Spider' seem peculiarly apt here. The last stanza moves into a subdued, deeply melancholy lament for the state of the world at present.

> Pity the planet, all joy gone
> from this sweet volcanic cone;
> peace to our children when they fall
> in small war on the heels of small
> war—until the end of time
> to police the earth, a ghost
> orbiting forever lost
> in our monotonous sublime.

'Fourth of July in Maine' is also discursive, continuing the use of Marvell's stanza pattern from 'The Garden' and 'Upon Appleton House' used in 'Waking Early Sunday Morning'. The inscription to Harriet Winslow is significant. On one level the poem is a Yeatsian or even Jonsonian house poem, celebrating a particular house and its traditions at a particular time and a particular place. But the poem is also partly, as Richard Fein has suggested,[3] Lowell's 'Prayer for his daughter', particularly in the second last part of the poem where his daughter, named after her aunt, becomes his image for the living continuity of tradition.

The poem falls naturally into three sections. The first four stanzas begin with an ironic though not savage evocation of a public event—the celebration of Independence Day on 4 July, with its small town parade commemorating the founding of the Republic, the United States of America with its bonded nationalities. This familiar Lowell approach helps link the past to the present, as the poet explores the meaning of continuity, the real significance of tradition. The dandyish Union Soldier (like the figure of Colonel Robert Shaw in 'For the Union Dead', or his declension in the same poem into 'the abstract Union soldier') represents values that seem more and more forgotten. 'Each child has won his blue / red, yellow ribbon'; and the blue is a reminder

3 Fein, *Robert Lowell*, p. 142.

of the whole of the American past—the Puritan ethos which stands so firmly behind the development of modern American capitalism (stanza four encapsulates ideas familiar from many of Lowell's poems—'Concord', 'Salem', 'At the Indian Killer's Grave', 'For the Union Dead', to mention only a few). There is the sense in these opening stanzas of the celebration as a rather absurd pantomime with little connection either with the past it celebrates or the present.

The next section, stanzas five to ten, celebrates the values represented by the white colonial frame house that once belonged to Harriet Winslow and which the poet now occupies. This is the personal American tradition represented by the house which embodies the best qualities of American civilisation:

> This white Colonial frame house,
> willed downwards, Dear, from you to us,
> still matters . . . .

It has a lived human significance as the product of a particular civilisation and a sort of act of faith. The house has a substantiality, a confidence and conviction in its shape and design that suggest some of the qualities of life in the past:

> The founders' faith was in decay,
> and yet their building seems to say:
> 'Every time I take a breath,
> my God you are the air I breathe.'

The house is an object of historical and religious significance, of a living, continuing tradition, unlike the annually and artificially revived Independence Day celebration.

The next four stanzas are addressed directly to Harriet Winslow herself. 'Dear Cousin', they begin. The character of the woman represents the spirit of the house and the poem stresses her living relationship to all aspects of the society around her: 'nurses, Negro, diplomat, down-easter, / cousins. . . . ' There is emphasis on her control ('kindly, majorfully directed') and on the central importance of the house and possessions themselves. Even in her illness away in Washington she kept in touch with them by phone, knowing more about the house and the whereabouts of objects in it than they did. Harriet Winslow is dead and is only remembered now as a name by a few old fossils; but the house remains, still representing continuity, though the garden and the barn are in decline.

In the last seven stanzas we have the emergence of the tradition into the present and a prayer for strength which this tradition alone is no longer strong enough to confer. The house will pass

on to his daughter and will help to give her personal indepen-
dence—the qualities and properties of Harriet Winslow herself—
a sense of proportion, friends, a house. The relatively long section
of two whole stanzas on the guinea-pigs conveys a sense of the
utter vulnerability, dispensability and disposability not only of the
animals but of all beings ('man and his poorest cousins') of this
generation as opposed to the centred and rather bossy control of
the aunt. There is the sense of the old attitudes no longer being
adequate to control or find one's place in reality. The daughter's
guinea pigs are described both ironically and tenderly in their
complex simplicity—their relation to the human world. They
simply exist, vulnerable, unattractive, content to praise through
their mere existence—'whatever stupor gave them breath / to
multiply before their death'. Like the skunks in 'Skunk Hour'
they represent animal vitality, the continuity of natural life, but
without the self-possession and the natural confident self-assertion
of the skunks themselves. The guinea-pigs are 'humble, giving,
idle, sensitive' and the opposite of nearly all these adjectives would
have to be applied to the skunks who 'will not scare'. One notices
too how the sound pattern unites the paradoxically and illuminat-
ingly combined words used for the guineapigs: 'untroubled petri-
fied, atremble'.

After this suggestion of the helplessness of the human state,
there is the sense of the influx of menacing force: ' . . . the north
wind rushes through / your ailing cedars, finds the gaps' and the
final scene evokes the present state of the family and the sense
almost of being beleaguered, 'food's lost sight of, dinner waits'.
There is a subtle contrast here with the aunt's ordered existence
with its place for drink ('fortified against the storm / by nightly
nips you once adored / though never going overboard') and music
so different from the broken routine and the stunned lethargy of
the present occupants:

> . . . dinner waits
> in the cold oven, icy plates—
> repeating and repeating, one
> Joan Baez on the gramophone.

It is interesting to note the range and character of Harriet
Winslow's favourite composers ('Monteverdi, Purcell, and Bach's
/ precursors' on the Magnavox) in comparison with the one hyp-
notic and monotonous record of Joan Baez on the gramophone,
a singer whose work combines nostalgia for the past and protest
against the present.

The final three stanzas convey a sense of lost innocence, with no energy or faith to control or order life, only enough to survive, to hold the family together. The final image is the one of keeping the fire burning, with its sense of the most primitive instinct for survival. This final double image of warmth and fire ('we escape the sun, rising and setting') suggests the larger forces of history as evoked in the opening description of the parade, and the smaller domestic fire ('We watch the logs fall. Fire once gone / we're done for') suggests the personal tradition as life-giving but now threatened. The poem ends with a prayer for strength from a greater force to face the demands of the personal life:

> Great ash and sun of freedom, give
> us this day the warmth to live,
> and face the household fire. We turn
> our backs, and feel the whiskey burn.

As so often in Lowell the end of summer and the approach of cold, the sense of domestic stagnation and fatigue at the end of day merge into a partly apocalyptic sense of the decline of the west, the decay of the simplicities of the past. There is a sense of continuity within history (the house, the American past), within the family (the poet's daughter), but there is too a sense of ageing, of diminishing resources.

'Central Park' is the most perfect poem in *Near the Ocean*, its exquisitely modulated unifying patterns, its subtly related images giving it a sense of organic wholeness and imaginative coherence unequalled by the other more expansive and ambitious Marvellian poems. It is a poem of complex, paradoxical symmetries, aimed like the other poems in the collection to show the state of human helplessness in front of violence and cruelty and the counter violence used to oppose it. The series of opposites and oppositions, relationships and equivalents, that the poem moves on, reveals the paradoxes of a society of violence and affluence— riches just out of reach, help which comes too late, strength which is weakness, positions of power which make their possessors weaker than ever, and under it all the metaphysical paradox of the human condition, torn between body and soul, life and death. The extraordinary achievement of this poem—and it is particularly remarkable when compared to the uncontained violence of earlier poems—is in the way Lowell is able to deal with these topics with full control of thought and feeling—to present a vision of violence and horror and to present it without revulsion or rejection or hysteria. Part of the impressive force of the poem comes from the effective use of incongruously tender words: 'each precious, pubic, public tangle' (like the 'sweet volcanic cone' of 'Waking Early Sunday Morning') which humanize and make more poignant the otherwise desolating or depersonalizing situation he is pointing to.

The poem's point of departure is a walk through Central Park, watching, looking at the bodies of lovers sunbaking in the grass. The emphasis on geometry and symmetry (the bodies like 'one figure of geometry, / multiplied to infinity', 'each precious, public, pubic tangle / an equilateral triangle') suggests the repetitious sameness of the human body, but also the sense of humiliation and limitation: 'The stain of fear and poverty / spread through each trapped anatomy'. The human beings are caught or trapped in their situation like the animals in the zoo of the park, like the lion drugged and humiliated by the smell. The sense of being deprived and starved spiritually and literally is shown to apply both to animal and human. The strongest animal (the lion) and the weakest (the newborn kitten) of the same species are unable to enjoy, or even survive by, the extravagant supplies which lie just out of reach. The poor young (lovers) and the rich old (Pharaohs) are equally helpless. The Pharaohs dying with banquets painted on their walls are linked (by the idea of food) with the young kitten dying with its food out of reach; silver foil and gold leaf are linked to each other and to 'spoil' and 'plunder', a useless abundance, suggesting in their different ways a sense of helpless mortality.[4] The attempt on the part of the Pharaohs to survive death merely added to their vulnerability: 'all your embalming left you mortal' and 'hideously eternal'.

The theme of helplessness before death leads into the last four lines—helplessness before the violence of life:

> We beg delinquents for our life.
> Behind each bush, perhaps a knife;
> each landscaped crag, each flowering shrub,
> hides a policeman with a club.

The violence is hidden behind the carefully controlled and tended (the *landscaped* crag, the *flowering* shrub). Patterns of light and darkness, shadow and sunshine move throughout; the opening image of the grounded kite connects with the later image of the snagged balloon and the fluttering paper kite. The sense of the touching frailty of human lust as a kind of spiritual aspiration—

> All wished to leave this drying crust,
> borne on the delicate wings of lust
> like bees, and cast their fertile drop
> into the overwhelming cup.

4 Cf. 'Rats' in *Notebook:* 'They died of starvation in a litter of food'.

—picks up the suggestions from the opening reference to 'light as pollen'; 'the stain of fear and poverty' is echoed later in the shadows that 'had stained the afternoon', while the small rocks, the 'shadow of some low stone', foreshadow the 'landscaped crag' of the last stanza and the 'dripping rock' behind which the abandoned kitten is found. Similarly the copy of Cleopatra's Needle brings in by association the reference to the Pharaohs and their rich, envied but vulnerable wealth. The poem demonstrates how everything moves around in an ironically vicious circle, and its control and unity serve to exacerbate the violence and helplessness of the central reality it depicts. It is an aspiration towards order, form, harmony, like the aspiration of the lovers depicted. But the poem shows, too, how peace is unavailable to the mind as it is permanently unavailable to the lovers this side of death; and the garden of Central Park with 'each landscaped crag', 'each flowering shrub' is no earthly paradise or garden of delights, but almost a parody of hell with violence, terror, decay and mortality suggested everywhere. It is the achievement of the poem that it is able to hold all these possibilities together in a structure of feeling that appals with its vision and delights with its management and control.

'Near the Ocean', the title poem of the collection, is the most obscure piece in the volume. It begins with the image of a severed head (one that occurs in several Lowell poems—'The Severed Head' and 'Florence', for instance), that has been identified as referring to Clytemnestra's words to Orestes, spoken to him when he is about to kill her. (Her words are quoted: 'Child, these breasts'.)[5] There is also a reference to Medusa and Perseus. The two opening stanzas seem to act out or suggest some violent domestic tension with murderous impulses presented in a mock-heroic way; it conveys the sense of some dominating power in the woman that both stifles and devours the man and against which he needs to react. The third stanza as they lie in bed 'near the ocean', used to suggest the presence of a primitive remnant of feeling in the relationship—the tyrant and tyrannicide image from the opening stanzas being related to the passion of the bridegroom and the bride, and both going back in their passion to prehistoric days.

The rest of the poem, following a movement not unlike that of 'Man and Wife' in *Life Studies*, recalls past incidents from their relationship. Throughout the remembered moments are recurrent motifs of dryness and its associations of sterility plus a sense of

5 See Cooper, *The Autobiographical Myth*, p. 136.

being worn away. The first memory recalls 'menstrual blood / *caking* the covers', 'the dry, childless Sunday walk' and 'steel and coal dust to land's end'. The second memory recalls how 'summer's coarse last quarter drought / had dried the hardveined elms'; there are references to 'gritty green' and how 'dehydration browned the grass'; and in the third image of sand—'sand, Atlantic Ocean, condoms, sand'—the idea of dryness and the idea of being worn down and worn away are combined in the image of sand. The tone here is one of exhaustion and stagnation, and the memories are of past corruption, past stagnation.

There are three precise memories evoked which seem to be or to contain betrayals: a moment at night in the New England countryside; waking on a Sunday morning in New York after a weekend of semi-riotous living; then a memory of years later in the same New England landscape with the elms now almost dried out in the drought-stricken landscape. The poem ends with a sense of relief in a prayer or recommendation to go to sleep. The presence of the sea is evoked and with it Lowell's final apostrophe —bracing, honest, unsentimental but full of a mature tenderness for his wife to whom the poem is both dedicated and addressed. The Medusa image returns, the knowledge of the possibility that this new attempt at human contact will again be petrified and fail, but there remains the strength to face this knowledge and yet to risk a human relationship—'a hand, your hand then! I'm afraid / to touch the crisp hair on your head— / Monster loved for what you are'.

In the final stanza we have once again the paradoxical finding of strength in an image of final decline (as in 'Skunk Hour' and 'Winter in Dunbarton' to mention only two other instances). Sand is an image of grinding down and destruction, but this process itself is ageless and unchanging and therefore has continuity and permanence: 'The ocean, grinding stones / can only speak the present tense'.

Notebook (1970)

Notebook in its revised edition (1970) consists of 373 unrhymed sonnets or quatorzains, written or rewritten between June 1967 and June 1970. Lowell, in an 'Afterthought', has said 'the poems in this book are written as one poem, intuitive in arrangement, but not a pile or sequence of related material'. He points out that the plot of the whole 'rolls with the seasons': 'The time is a summer, an autumn, a winter, a spring, another summer. . . . I have flashbacks to what I remember, and fables inspired by impulse. Accident threw up subjects, and the plot swallowed them— famished for human chances.'

Lowell claimed that the poems in *Notebook* are written as one poem, doubtless with the example of John Berryman in mind; but where Berryman in *The Dream Songs* uses the persona of Henry to organize and focus the whole, Lowell projects himself and aspects of his own life to give the work its central unity. In his 'Afterthought' Lowell comments: '*Notebook* is less an almanack than the story of my life. Many events turn up, many others of equal or greater personal reality do not. *This is not my private lash, or confession, or a puritan's too literal pornographic honesty, glad to share secret embarrassment and triumph.*' (My italics.)

As with *Life Studies* one senses that *Notebook* is a unified work; but it is longer, more haphazard and random than *Life Studies* and its structure is not reducible to clear patterns. John Fuller[1] has said that Lowell calls *Notebook* a poem rather than a sequence because 'one imagines that he merely wishes to deny the particular discreteness for so long presumed to be characteristic of short poems in modern collections', while Jonathan Raban has remarked[2] that *Notebook* looks back to the Elizabethan sonnet sequence and sideways to the novel. This suggests its paradoxical characteristics of contrivance, imitation and translation, freedom, spontaneity and ease. These poems reflect the whole spectrum of a full life and have both the disparate breadth of the totality and

1 *The Sonnet*, London 1972, p. 47.
2 *The Society of the Poem*, London 1971, p. 152.

the unifying reduction of the centrality from which they spring. *Notebook* creates the illusion of presenting the high points of an active life, its public and private concerns, travel in different countries (Mexico, Brazil, England), love affairs, student days, teaching, participating in daily social, political and literary activities; the persona's different roles as student, father, husband, lover, poet. The immense range of the whole is augmented by an abundance of literary, artistic, political, and historical references moving throughout—drawing on his reading, his knowledge of his family, the history of his country and the world. It is not a wilful display of knowledge for knowledge's sake, or a demonstration of the persona's grip on *Kulturgeschichte*, but an indication of the aliveness and relevance of the past for a richly informed mind bringing all its responses to bear on the tensions of the present.

The various attempts that have so far been made to indicate the scope of the whole do not give nearly a rich enough idea of its variety. The danger of indicating lines of development and control is that they may suggest too schematic a pattern, too rigid a design; on the other hand to ignore these is to miss the sense of organic unity of the whole. There are sections within *Notebook* which have a firm development and organization. The poems in 'Long Summer', 'Through the Night' and 'Charles River' are not only unified by a locality or mood, but stand in a particular relationship to each other. Other sections—'Mexico', 'Writers', 'The Powerful'—consist of independent poems related by a theme. Other sections group together poems which have no apparent relationship on any level. One moves through this book as through a city, at times oriented by familiar landmarks, at others surrounded by the unfamiliar, yet having always a sense of life circulating around and defined by certain areas of concern and perception.

What strikes one about *Notebook* is the way it has all the contents and concerns of high poetry, but without the tones or the formality or the formalizing tendencies of the earlier work. The best of the individual sonnets are highly wrought, and often difficult and allusive like the earlier work, but they are not overwrought. They convey a forceful impression of freedom and ease, while detailed analysis reveals how impressively organized the best are. At their weakest—as in some of the poems in 'February and March' or 'A Souvenir' or 'For Eugene McCarthy', or 'Letter with Poems for a Letter with Poems' or 'To John Berryman'—the poems can give the sense of elliptical private notes, dashed down to capture a sensation or impression, but not sufficiently shaped and processed to become communicable. This sense of non-communication in a few poems is reflected in a certain flatness and roughness in the language.

Notebook is in a real sense Lowell's notebook. The placing of poems and incidents suggests the day to day quality of the whole. Like many another journal or workbook it contains multiple cross-references to other aspects of the writer's life and work. One of the pleasures *Notebook* gives is that of settling into a known world with old landmarks seen in a new light. I am thinking here of quite simple things: to take two examples from the opening pages. —Poem 3 in the first section 'Harriet' reminds one in essential imagery of 'Soft Wood' in *For the Union Dead*; likewise poem 1 in 'Long Summer' of 'The Drinker' from *For the Union Dead*; while No 2 inevitably recalls the setting, décor and themes of some of the personal poems in *Near the Ocean*. There are many other examples which draw on the same fields of imagery and reference as other Lowell poems. And of course there are the imitations. Translations have always been a feature of Lowell's output; they occur in *Poems*; there is a whole book— *Imitations*—devoted to them; more than half of *Near the Ocean* consists of translations. In *Notebook*, hitherto unidentified imitations occur: 'Le Cygne' (from Mallarmé) and 'Volveran'—a wholly convincing and, at the same time, wholly original rendering since it so forcefully changes the form but not the feeling of Bécquer's *Volverán las oscuras golondrinas*, using it to refer to a love situation. 'Die Gold-Orangen' is similarly a completely personal version of Goethe's 'Mignon's Lied' which however remains remarkably true to the rhythmic movement and nostalgic disorientation of the original. The opening of 'Revenant' (May, No 13) is a very modern version of Hölderlin's 'Hälfte des Lebens', remarkably close to the pitch and cadence of the original. The idea of Hölderlin's title is one which is present in many of these poems. 'End of the Saga' uses details from the end of the *Nibelungenlied*, Kriemhild's massacre of her enemies, and juxtaposes it without comment with 'Deutschland über Alles' which gives a view of the demented corruption of Nazi Germany.

More numerous than the imitations are the quotations or revisions and recastings of earlier poems: 'In the Cage'; 'Mania in Buenos Aires, 1962', 'Night Sweat', 'Caligula' and 'Water 1948'. The two poems, 'For Theodore Roethke' and '1958' ('Remember standing with me in the dark') are taken over from *Near the Ocean*; other poems contain cross-references or partial allusions to other earlier Lowell poems. For instance Poem 4 in Charles River 'There was rebellion, Father, when the door slammed' is a rewrite of 'Rebellion' from *Poems 1938-1949* ('There was rebellion, father, when the mock / French windows slammed . . . '). 'The Flaw' (No 3 in the section 'The Races') develops images and ideas contained in the piece by the same title in *For the Union Dead*, and 'Waterloo' is related to the early poem 'Buttercups'. It is not always possible to see what improvement, if any, the change of verse form has made. In some cases one feels the poet is rather ruthlessly exploiting and processing his own work, especially as the sonnet flattens out various earlier forms. John Bayley in an important review commented on this very point, 'Poems like cars go back to the crusher',[3] using an image and idea derived from Lowell himself, who writes in 'The Nihilist as Hero': 'Life by definition breeds on change, / each season we scrap new cars and wars and women'.

The historical reality of the events is emphasized by the unusual number of dates in the titles of the poems. Lowell's concern with the structure or the informational substructure of *Notebook* is further borne out by the list of dates he appends to the volume. This list includes the Vietnam War, the Arab-Israeli Six Days War, the Pentagon March, Martin Luther King's murder, Robert Kennedy's murder, the Russian Occupation of Czechoslovakia. *Notebook* is in a sense a documentary poem; but the references to world events are on the whole oblique. They show the scope, variety and contemporaneity of the whole, but these have always been features of Lowell's work; it is the proliferation of these references in a single book that impresses, and helps to define attitude and approach. What really moves one are not the events or references themselves, but the way they are shown to have impact on the sensibility of the persona of Lowell who projects himself in a variety of guises and roles in every aspect of everyday life.

Notebook is protean, loose and baggy. In appropriating the everyday to form the roughage of the poem, Lowell uses conversations and gossip overheard; he transcribes and transposes letters received, sometimes from writers, at other times from strangers or people known at a particular phase of his life; he absorbs pieces and fragments from his reading (in this collage method the influence and example of Pound and Williams were no doubt important). He refers to people met in passing in an attempt to convey some of the sense of the pressure of life, its intensity and the feel of things that have impact on the poet's mind.

Like an Elizabethan sonneteer (and like Berryman again) Lowell constantly reflects on the nature of his art, writing sonnets

3 *The Review*, No. 24, December 1970, p. 4.

about his writing. Poems about reading his own work, or about being recognized in public as the figure he has become, need placing against a piece like 'Publication Day'—a poem made out of pieces of a letter received from a woman who has had a book rejected. The fact that such poems recur throughout and are not grouped as a separate cycle suggests the continuing preoccupation, the nature of the worried concern. Lowell takes his public status as a poet for granted; he does not try to ignore it or overemphasize it; he explores it rather than exploits it. The ending of *Les Mots*, for instance, reveals his concern with the nature of what he is doing:

> Is it refusal of error breaks a life—
> the supreme artist, Flaubert, was a boy before
> the mania for phrases dried his heart

These lines need to be related to the end of poem 4 in 'Long Summer': 'most things worth doing are worth doing badly'—a line too worried in its context to be smug or complacent. Such lines recur as an apology for his making. This preoccupation is not the Yeatsian antithesis of perfection of the life or of the work, but a realization that such an antithesis is false, that the quality of the life and of the art must somehow go together. So he writes in 'To Margaret Fuller Drowned': 'progress is not by renunciation'; and in 'Henry and Waldo': 'few lives contained so many renunciations. / Thoreau, like Mallarmé and many another, / found life too brief for perfection and long for comfort.' The idea that the perfection of the work is escaping him is returned to constantly.

This acute concern seems to go with the openness of the form to the random quality of life: the poem as moment rather than as monument. It is also related to one of the most problematical issues of the later Lowell—his concern to bring poetry into relationship with prose, his statement that he no longer knows the difference between prose and verse,[4] his ambitious need to align the poem with the novel. Lowell's need not to sacrifice reality to some extreme view of perfection means that he constantly runs the risk of being random, even sometimes slapdash. The need to appropriate the contingent can work against the feeling of the concrete in a poem as a whole and the belief that 'nothing is real until set down in words' can lead to the gigantism that Lowell deplores elsewhere.

That *Notebook* has an organization and a structure lengthy and

---

4 See D. S. Carne-Ross, 'Conversation with Robert Lowell', *Delos 1*, 1968, p. 165.

leisurely examination and analysis alone can demonstrate. But it is clear that a few large themes and preoccupations hold the whole together. They are time and memory, the relationship between age and youth, and above all the always present spectre of death, the constant intimations of mortality; the hero; the artist; and love in all its aspects from a savage, often rather adolescent eroticism to the resigned maturity of 'We are all here for such a short time / we might as well be good to one another'. There are constant preoccupations with life and art, loneliness and communication, 'rot and renewal', 'vacations, stagnant growth', 'continuities and discontinuities'. There are related images of stars and water, winter and cities, fish and animals, stones and flowers, images of Eden and Hell. Peculiarly personal motifs recur and set up emotional reverberations—window, wall, grass, leaf, the moon, and, most insistently recurrent but without thematic development, the motif of blood, which occurs in forty poems. Also threading through the book are characteristic colours—white, yellow, blue, red and, most important, green. More consistently than the other colours, green, which appears in fifty-three poems, is used not only realistically and impressionistically, but also expressionistically, charged with a mood or state. It has sometimes the obvious association of freshness and greenness, but more often an overtone of the sinister and brutal—'the green steel head' in 'The March'; 'green mustache' ('Charles Russell Lowell: 1835-1864'); there are 'the greens washed to double greenness' and 'a . . . greenly brutal quarry' of the poems 'In the Forties'. Images of evanescence, fragility and purity are played off against images of vitality and vigour, filth and fertility, the cruelty and continuity of nature. The recurrent concern of the relationship between strength and weakness, the real nature of heroism, is bound into the overriding concern with extremism in all its forms, the point at which the heroic or noble corrupts into its opposite. Associative ideas and patterns, small pools and clusters of themes gather across and through groups of poems: the theme of mass murder mentioned in 'End of the Saga', 'Hell' and 'Rats' and 'The River God' is linked by association in the same group of poems with the theme of overpopulation, pollution and overcrowding, while explorations of the relationship between body and mind bring in associations of brainwashing and other totalitarian means of taking over individual identity and responsibility. The extermination of the Jews mentioned in 'Deutschland über Alles' prepares us for the association made in 'The River God' between Mao's extermination of lepers and the ancient Aztec rites of human sacrifice. Even across a small group of poems, these interrelationships serve to illustrate

116

Lowell's belief in the 'eternal return', the source of the book's unity as a whole.

It is significant that some of the best poems in *Notebook* are about other writers. Many of these poems are aristocratic in their celebration of the role of the writer, but the tone is all important: these writers were friends, often very close ones, and some of the poems grapple with complex emotions. They do not stand off at a distance and celebrate a role, they remember a relationship; so that while the poems mention people who are widely known as writers they are poems not about being a writer but about what it means to be a human being. All these poems are remarkable for their humanity, warmth and candour, their intensely sympathetic sense of fellow feeling. The number of poems addressed to or commemorating various writers of his own time is particularly striking. Among Lowell's contemporaries, or seniors or friends, Mary McCarthy, Randall Jarrell, Peter Taylor, T. S. Eliot, Ezra Pound, Ford Madox Ford, Allen Tate, William Carlos Williams, Robert Frost, F. O. Mathiessen, Norman Mailer, Theodore Roethke, Elizabeth Bishop, John Berryman have sections or poems named directly after them; I. A. Richards, Louis MacNeice and John Crowe Ransom have poems dedicated to them or feature in poems under different titles. Among the established classics of the past, Sir Thomas More, Thoreau, Emerson, Milton, Coleridge, Rimbaud, Sappho and Marlowe are the subjects of poems named after them, while Flaubert and Mallarmé, to take two examples only, feature in poems to illustrate the extreme dedication of their lives to and the consequent increasing desiccation of their art. Purity and perfection seem to drive away personality and power.

Lowell's concern with his own status as a poet, with his own role in society as a participant in public affairs is central to *Notebook*. He is as aware of his fame and his social place in *Notebook* as he is of the role of his family in *Life Studies*. It would be false humility and self-defeating not to project this part of his image. But Lowell is concerned to overcome the twin dangers that have beset the poet in modern times—that of becoming hermetically sealed off and withdrawn from his society in the perfectionist pursuit of his art—or that of becoming too closely involved with its transient issues: becoming either its prophet or its journalist. Even an unselfconscious poem about reading his own work recognizes the various dangers involved in fame, the threats to real achievement and fulfilment. Throughout *Notebook* there is the restless circling around questions, the facing of issues without a too facile commitment to one side or the other. It is interesting that the image and the motif of circles, itself the title of a separate group of poems within the book, is one that unifies *Notebook* as a whole.

One of the central concerns of *Notebook* is the conflict between the personal and the public life. This emerges not only in the poems about writing but, even more insistently, in the political poems which seek for a way to understand the violence of political events and their relationship to the private life. A very large number of the poems in *Notebook* deal with political and historical experience: 'October and November' deals with the turbulent public and political life of the sixties in the U.S.A.; 'The Powerful' covers a wide spectrum of historical reference, but each poem deals with violence and death, and attitudes to these. Throughout there is concern with resolution, an attempted harmony of opposites, the search for the golden mean. 'Too far is easy; enough a miracle' as he writes in 'Trunks' ('Circles : 9'). This is closely related to the theme that recurs in the political poems and the poems on literature and art: the dangers of both withdrawal and over-commitment.

> Is it worse to choke on the vomit of cowardice,
> or blow the world up on a point of honor?

he asks in the poem 'Munich 1938', a fine sonnet whose final octave is devoted to an evocation of John Crowe Ransom

> John Crowe Ransom at Kenyon College, Gambier, Ohio,
> looking at primitive African art on loan:
> gleam-bottomed naked warriors of oiled brown wood,
> makeshift tin straws in their hands for spears;
> far from the bearded, armored, all-profile hoplite
> on the Greek vase; not distant maybe in their gods—
> John saying, 'Well, they may not have been good neighbours,
> but they never troubled the rest of the world.'

Here a personal image of a friend relates the idea of war and conflict within a small circle to the involvement of the whole modern world in the political consequences and the historical ramifications of all political decisions. The theme of cowardice returns in 'The March' poems I and II, based on the famous march on the Pentagon. The poems focus on the confrontation between the two groups involved, the human, puny protestors and the robot-like steel army. The first poem is filled with the wild elation of a momentary human solidarity asserting itself against the inhuman monumentality of politics:

> Under the too white marmoreal Lincoln Memorial,
> the too tall marmoreal Washington Obelisk . . .
> lovely to lock arms, to march absurdly locked. . . .

In the second poem this elation has drained away in the reality of pain, fear and defeat. This bungling and broken heroism is in contrast to the complete heroism, with its element of self-effacing generosity, of a figure like Charles Russell Lowell, celebrated in the next poem: 'He had, *gave* everything'. Something of an ideal of heroism emerges in the next poem, 'Caracas II':

> one could get through life, though mute, with courage
> and a merciful heart—two things, and a third thing:
> humour. . . .

These perhaps are qualities which determine the attitudes of poems like 'The March' and help the poet to avoid extremes.

A similarly self-questioning activity can be observed in the many poems devoted to writers and artists and poets. The Renaissance idea of the survival of memory or incident through art is taken up directly and indirectly in a number of poems; but this sense of endurance and survival through art is played off against the sense that all is destructible; all is expendable. One last poem will serve to illustrate this and related points. 'Reading Myself'

> Like millions, I took just pride and more than just,
> first striking matches that brought my blood to boiling;
> I memorized tricks to set the river on fire,
> somehow never wrote something to go back to.
> Even suppose I had finished with wax flowers
> and earned a pass to the minor slopes of Parnassus . . .
> No honeycomb is built without a bee
> adding circle to circle, cell to cell,
> the wax and honey of a mausoleum—
> this round dome proves its maker is alive,
> the corpse of such insect lives preserved in honey,
> prays that the perishable work live long
> enough for the sweet-tooth bear to desecrate—
> this open book . . . my open coffin.

In this poem Lowell looks back over his own career, weighing the kind of poetry he did write from his first highly formalist phase— 'I memorised tricks to set the river on fire'—against the kind of poetry he conceivably might have written—highly aesthetic minor poetry aiming at beauty rather than the ragged energy and vitality of life. But Lowell realizes that a life's work, a honeycomb, is only built by painstaking and humble labour in a series of small per- fected stages: 'No honeycomb is built without a bee / adding circle to circle, cell to cell'. Yet the perfected life's work becomes 'the wax and honey of a mausoleum', paradoxically proving the bee's vitality. The life of the bee goes into the making of the honey, and all that one can hope for is that the honey will survive long enough for the sweet-tooth bear—the reader—to draw sustenance from it. This open book (his open life, with all its confessions, moments, revelations) is his open coffin, and is Lowell's way of asserting that his art and his life are one. The poem is particularly related to an earlier piece in 'My Death':

> Reading this book to four or five that night
> at Cuernavaca, till the lines glowered and glowed,
> and my friend, Monsignor Illich, ascetic donkey,
> braying, 'Will you die, when the book is done?'
> It stopped my heart, and not my mouth. I said,
> 'I have begun to wonder.'

It is Lowell's way of showing how the deepest values of art are inseparable from those of life.

Lowell ends his 'Afterthought' to *Notebook* with the words: 'In truth I seem to have felt mostly the joys of living; in remembering, in recording, thanks to the gift of the Muse, it is the pain'. But the last words of *Notebook* should be those of the last poem 'Obit', and they are a moving affirmation of life in all its incompleteness and transience:

> . . . I'm for and with myself in my otherness,
> in the eternal return of earth's fairer children,
> the lily, the rose, the sun on dusk and brick,
> the loved, the lover, and their fear of life,
> their unconquered flux, insensate oneness, their painful 'it was . . . '

SELECT BIBLIOGRAPHY

A. Editions

Land of Unlikeness, Cummington 1944.
Lord Weary's Castle, New York 1946.
Poems, 1938-1949, London 1950.
This English edition includes poems from *Land of Unlikeness, Lord Weary's Castle* and *The Mills of the Kavanaughs*.
The Mills of the Kavanaughs, New York 1951.
Life Studies, London and New York 1959.
The London edition did not include the prose essay '91 Revere Street' until the edition of 1968.
Imitations, New York 1961, London 1963.
Phaedra, New York 1961, London 1963.
For the Union Dead, New York 1964, London 1965.
The Old Glory, New York 1965, London 1966.
Near the Ocean, New York and London 1967.
Prometheus Bound, New York 1969, London 1970.
Notebook 1967-68, New York 1969.
The Voyage, New York and London 1969.
Notebook (revised and enlarged edition), London 1970.
History, New York and London 1973.
For Lizzie and Harriet, New York and London 1973.
The Dolphin, New York and London 1973.

Secondary Works

Cooper, Philip, *The Autobiographical Myth of Robert Lowell*. Chapel Hill 1970.
Explores Lowell's poetry as a single body of work. Extremely valuable for identification of sources in a miscellaneous selection of poems.
Cosgrave, Patrick, *The Public Poetry of Robert Lowell*. London 1970.
Controversial and stimulating study of Lowell's development.
Fein, Richard J., *Robert Lowell*. New York 1970.
Covers all of the work except for *Notebook*.
London, Michael and Boyers, Robert (eds), *Robert Lowell: A Portrait of the Artist in his Time*. New York 1970.
A valuable collection of essays and review articles. Complete bibliography by Jerome Mazzaro of all articles on Lowell from 1938-69.

Mazzaro, Jerome, *The Poetic Themes of Robert Lowell.* University of Michigan 1965.
Indispensable, pioneer study; largely thematic approach from the Catholic point of view.

Martin, Jay, *Robert Lowell.* University of Minnesota Pamphlets on American Writers.
Brief but thorough introduction in a standard and established series.

Mciners, R. K., *Everything to be endured: An Essay on Robert Lowell and Modern Poetry.* University of Missouri Press 1970.
First study of influence of Allen Tate on Lowell. Important observations on a few poems and stimulating insights on Lowell's work as a whole.

Staples, Hugh, *Robert Lowell: The First Twenty Years.* London 1962.
Pioneer study of Lowell's work up to *Life Studies.* Includes bibliography of Lowell's writings 1939-61 and the text of the poem *The Mills of the Kavanaughs.*

C. Articles and Other Papers

Alvarez, A., *The Shaping Spirit.* London 1958.

——, *Beyond All This Fiddle.* London 1968.

——, 'Robert Lowell in Conversation with A. Alvarez'. *The Review,* 8, August 1963, 36-40.

——, 'A Talk with Robert Lowell'. *Encounter,* XXIV, February 1965, 39-43.

Bayley, John, 'Robert Lowell: The Poetry of Cancellation'. *London Magazine,* VI, June 1966, 77-85.

——, 'The King as Commander' (review of *Notebook*). *The Review,* 24, December 1970, 3-7.

Bowen, Roger, 'Confession and Equilibrium: Robert Lowell's Poetic Development'. *Criticism,* XI, 1969, 78-93.

Brooks, Cleanth and Penn Warren, Robert, *Conversations on the Craft of Poetry.* New York 1961.

Buckley, V., 'Trial and Error: The Poetry of Robert Lowell', *Quadrant,* January-February 1970, 20-31.

Calhoun, Richard J., 'The Poetic Metamorphosis of Robert Lowell'. *Furman Studies,* XIII, 1, 7-17.

——, 'Lowell's "My Last Afternoon with Uncle Devereux Winslow"'. *Explicator,* XXIII, January 1965, 38.

Cambon, Glauco, *The Inclusive Flame: Studies in American Poetry.* Bloomington 1963.

Carne-Ross, D. S., 'Conversation with Robert Lowell'. *Delos,* I, 1968, 165-75.

Doherty, Paul C., 'The Poet as Historian: "For the Union Dead" by Robert Lowell'. *Concerning Poetry,* I, Fall 1968, 37-41.

Donoghue, Dennis, *Connoisseurs of Chaos.* London 1966.

Edwards, Thomas R., *Imagination and Power: A Study of Poetry on Public Themes.* London 1971.

Ehrenpreis, Irvin, 'The Age of Lowell', in Irvin Ehrenpreis (ed.), *American Poetry*. London 1965, pp. 68-95.

Giovannini, G., 'Lowell's After Surprising Conversions'. *The Explicator*, IX, June 1951, Comment 53.

Gross, Harvey, *Sound and Form in Modern Poetry: A Study of Prosody from Thomas Hardy to Robert Lowell*. Ann Arbor 1964.

Hamilton, Ian (ed.), *The Modern Poet*. London 1968.

Hardison, O. B. Jr, 'Robert Lowell: The Poet and the World's Body'. *Shenandoah*, XIV, Winter 1963, 24-32.

Hill, Geoffrey, 'Robert Lowell: "Contrasts and Repetitions"'. *Essays in Criticism*, XIII, 1963, 188-197.

Hoffman, Daniel, 'Robert Lowell's *Near the Ocean*: The Greatness and Horror of Empire'. *Hollins Critic*, IV, February 1967, 1-16.

Holloway, John, 'Robert Lowell and the Public Dimension'. *Encounter*, XXX, April 1968, 73-9.

Jarrell, Randall, *Poetry and the Age*. New York 1955.

——, *The Third Book of Criticism*. New York 1969.

Leibowitz, Herbert, 'Robert Lowell: Ancestral Voices'. *Salmagundi*, I, 4, 1966-7, 25-43.

Luytens, D. B., *The Creative Encounter*. London 1960.

Malouf, D., *Poetry at the Seventies*. Current Affairs Bulletin, University of Sydney, August 1970.

Mailer, Norman, *The Armies of the Night*. New York 1968.

Mazzaro, Jerome, 'Robert Lowell's Early Politics of Apocalypse', in Jerome Mazzaro (ed.), *Modern American Poetry: Essays in Criticism*. New York 1970.

——, 'Robert Lowell and the Kavanaugh Collapse'. *University of Windsor Review*, 5, 1969-70, pp. 1-24.

——, 'Lowell After *For the Union Dead*'. *Salmagundi*, I, 4, 1966-7, pp. 57-68.

McAleer, John T., 'Lowell's "Mary Winslow"'. *Explicator*, XVIII, February 1960, 29.

McCormick, John, 'Falling Asleep over Grillparzer. An Interview with Robert Lowell'. *Poetry*, LXXXI, 1953, 269-79.

Miller, Terry, 'The Prosodies of Robert Lowell'. *Speech Monographs*, XXXV, November 1968, 425-34.

Naipaul, V. S., 'Et in America Ego: Conversation with Robert Lowell'. *Listener*, 4 September 1969.

Ostroff, Anthony, 'On Robert Lowell's "Skunk Hour"'. *The Contemporary Poet as Artist and Critic*. Boston 1964.

Parkinson, Thomas (ed.), *Robert Lowell: A Collection of Critical Essays*. Englewood Cliffs 1968.

——, 'For the Union Dead'. *Salmagundi*, I, 4, 1966-7, 87-96.

Pearson, Gabriel, 'Robert Lowell'. *The Review*, 20 March 1969, 3-36. (Reprinted in Martin Dodsworth (ed.), *The Survival of Poetry*, London 1970.)

Perloff, Marjorie, 'Death by Water: The Winslow Elegies of Robert Lowell'. *English Literary History*, XXXIV, 1967, 116-40.

——, 'Realism and the Confessional Mode of Robert Lowell'. *Contemporary Literature*, XI, Autumn 1970, 470-87.

Raban, Jonathan, *The Society of the Poem*. London 1971.

Ricks, C., 'Authority in Poems'. *Southern Review*, V, 1969, 203-8.

——, 'The Three Lives of Robert Lowell', (review of *For the Union Dead*). *New Statesman*, 26 March 1965.

Rink, Sister Mary Terese, 'The Sea in Lowell's "Quaker Graveyard in Nantucket" '. *Renascence*, XX, 1967, 39-43.

Seidel, Frederick, 'Robert Lowell', in *Writers at Work: The Paris Review Interviews, Second Series*. New York 1963. (Reprinted in T. Parkinson, *Robert Lowell*.)

Stallworthy, Jon, 'W. B. Yeats and the Dynastic Theme'. *Critical Quartrely*, VII, Autumn 1965, 247-65.

Standenwick, Desales, 'Notes on Robert Lowell'. *Renascence*, VIII, 1955-6, 75-83.

Staples, Hugh B., 'Beyond Charles River to the Acheron: An Introduction to the Poetry of Robert Lowell'. *Poets in Progress*, Evanston 1967.

——, 'A Graph of Revelations. An Introduction to the Poetry of Robert Lowell'. *Northwestern University Tri-quarterly*, Winter 1959, p. 7-12.

Times Literary Supplement, Review of *Poems 1939-1949* and *Life Studies*, 14 October 1960.

Trilling, Lionel, *The Experience of Literature: A Reader with Commentaries*. New York 1967.

Wallace-Crabbe, C., 'Robert Lowell's Version of History'. *Westerly*, April 1969, 37-44.

Wiebe, Dallas E., 'Mr. Lowell and Mr. Edwards'. *Wisconsin Studies in Contemporary Literature*, III, Spring-Summer 1962, 21-31.